Cambridge Regional Geogr

Editors **Harry Tolley,** *School of Education, U*
Keith Orrell, *Department of Education*

The East Midlands

Frank Molyneux
Associate Lecturer, School of Education, University of Nottingham

David Dwelly
Head of Geography, Wilsthorpe School, Long Eaton

Published by the Press Syndicate of the University of Cambridge
The Pitt Building, Trumpington Street, Cambridge CB2 1RP
40 West 20th Street, New York, NY 10011–4211, USA
10 Stamford Road, Oakleigh, Victoria 3166, Australia

© Cambridge University Press 1992

First published 1992

Printed in Malta by Interprint Limited

A catalogue record for this book is available from the British Library.

ISBN 0 521 27498 2

Acknowledgements
The authors are grateful to many people and organisations in the East Midlands who have provided a wealth of material, skills and support in producing this book. Much is owed to the planning officers and elected representatives of the ten major local authorities for their willingness to share their particular professional expertise and insight into the region and its development. We are grateful to many at the Flying Training School, RAF Cranwell, particularly Wing Commander W. M. N. Cross and Flt.-Lieut. S. Biglands. Personal thanks are due to the following: Allan Ainsworth, Steve Biglands, Peter Brown, Michael Cross, Colin Dwelly, Tim Heeley, Mike Henshall, Roger Jones, June Lemon, Irving and Verit Mayers, John Pirt, Mieke van Nunen, Elaine Watts, John Winder, Owen Wood and Steve Worthington. The publishers would like to thank the following for permission to use particular items. Photographs: p.8 Peter Arkell; p.10 A. M. Allain; p.29 *The Lincolnshire Echo*; p.32 Post Syndication; p.51 East Midlands International Airport; p.87 D. Bennett; (all other photographs are the authors'). Extracts: p.9 from Hoskins, *East Midlands and the Peak*. Harper Collins Publishers; p.41 by courtesy of the *Yorkshire Post*.

Contents

1 English Shires or the East Midlands? 5
2 People and places – past and present 13
3 Rocks, rivers and resources 23
4 Rocks, riches and renewal 35
5 Water, wheels and wings 45
6 Ploughs, profits and politics 54
7 Changing patterns and places of work 61
8 Central places and rural spaces 69
9 Land for living and leisure 79
10 A choice of futures – a future of choices? 90

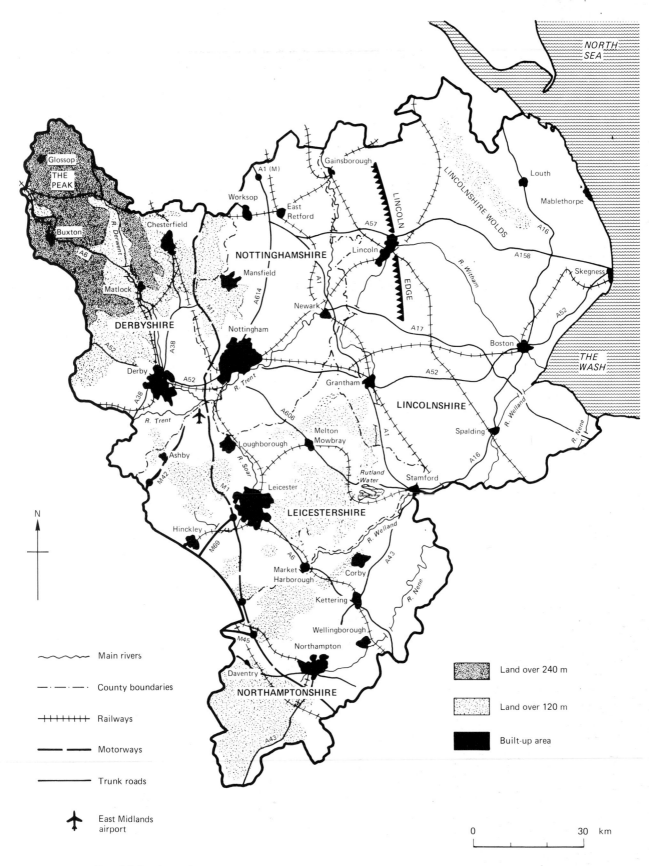

Fig. 1.1. *The East Midlands region*.

1 English Shires or the East Midlands?

Fig. 1.2. *The Standard Regions*.
Source: Central Statistical Office.

Central Statistical Office (CSO)
A branch of the Cabinet Office responsible for collecting and presenting statistics from all government departments. Its publications are valuable to geographers.

data
Known facts, including numbers, which serve as the starting points for measuring and reasoning in geography. The word is the plural of *datum* (Latin). For example, datum level is the agreed sea level from which all land heights and sea depths are measured.

formal region
An area containing sets of geographical features that distinguish it from surrounding areas.

functional region
An area we can recognise by some human activity organised within it.

The area covered by this book is shown in Fig. 1.1. The five counties of the East Midlands – Derbyshire, Leicestershire, Lincolnshire, Northamptonshire and Nottinghamshire – are described by the East Midlands Tourist Board (EMTB) as 'the English Shires'. But the government has divided the country into Standard Regions to help with planning and management (see Fig. 1.2). This raises an important question: 'What is the East Midlands?'

The **Central Statistical Office (CSO)** uses the Standard Regions for collecting and publishing **data**. Accurate data are essential for the efficient running of any country and are very valuable in geography. We can use CSO data to learn about the East Midlands, which is one of eight Standard Regions in England. Each region contains several counties which are our largest local government units. In Northern Ireland the units are called boards; in Scotland they are local authority regions. There are also smaller local government units – cities, boroughs, districts and parishes.

> Look carefully at the map of Standard Regions on Fig. 1.2. The East Midlands is labelled. Use your atlas to name the other regions, and the cities marked by dots.

There are regions and regions

There are several areas in Britain where certain features go together. Your atlas will show the Highlands of Scotland, the Lake District and the Fens. Other areas have concentrations of activities. These give us regional names like 'The Potteries' and 'The Black Country'. In geography we call these **formal regions**. The East Midlands is not a formal region – it is too varied.

So the East Midlands region is a group of five counties linked together for particular purposes. In geography we call such areas **functional regions**. They are set up by different organisations for various purposes and are of many sizes. The functional region of the East Midlands cuts into and across formal regions like the Peak District and the Fens. Figure 1.3 shows some of the functional regions used by British Telecom in the 1980s, and Fig. 1.4 outlines the principal local authority areas. These remind us that regions change with human activities. Even landscapes are altered as new technology changes our lifestyles and living space. Certainly the East Midlands is changing. By studying its geography we aim to understand these changes better.

Fig. 1.3. *British Telecom phone book areas.* (below)
Source: British Telecom.

Fig. 1.4. *Local authority areas of the East Midlands.* (right)
Source: Trent Geographer, **9–10**, 1986.

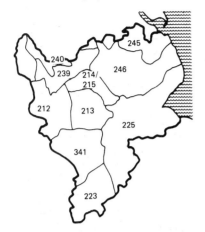

212 Derby and District	240 Sheffield and Rotherham
213 Nottingham and District	245 South Humberside and North Lincolnshire
214/215 Mansfield, Newark and Districts	246 Mid-Lincolnshire
223 Northampton	341 Leicester and District
225 Peterborough	
239 Chesterfield, Worksop and Hope Valley	

electoral register
All heads of households in the UK are required by law to complete forms from which lists of adults entitled to vote are compiled. Electoral registers or rolls are valuable sources of data in geography.

Parties, politics and power

All local authorities consist of councils elected by the adults living in the area who are on the **electoral register**. Central government is also elected by voters from particular areas. Members of Parliament (MPs) represent parliamentary constituencies. These are not the same as the local government areas (Fig. 1.4). Figure 1.5 shows the parliamentary constituencies of the East Midlands, and the political parties of the MPs elected in June 1987.

1 Find out in which local government units you live.
2 Make a list of all the councillors who represent you, the councils on which they serve, and any political parties to which they may belong.
3 Write to one of your local councillors and your MP asking them to describe their work.
4 Use Fig. 1.5 to describe the pattern of the 1987 General Election results in the East Midlands.

Regional trends

Using CSO data, we can compare regions and ask whether the East Midlands is distinctive or stands out in any way. The East Midlands can be ranked within the eight English regions to form a geographical league table. For example: 'The East Midlands is the third largest region by area but the sixth by population'.

Study Table 1.1.
1 Rank the East Midlands within England for main types of occupations in 1984.
2 Describe and try to explain the main variations in work patterns across the region.

Fig. 1.5. *Parliamentary constituencies and results of the 1987 General Election.*

Source: Reproduced from *The Times Guide to the House of Commons*, 1987, by kind permission of Times Books.

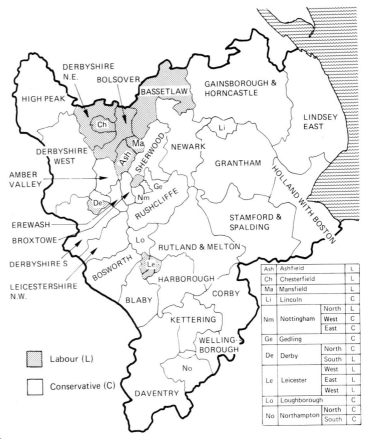

Table 1.1 *Regional and county data, 1984–86*

Regions/Counties	Area (thousand km²)	Popn 1986 (millions)	Occupations 1984 – % employees in			
			Agric. 1	Energy 2	Manuf. 3	Services 4
East Midlands	15.6	3.9	2.3	5.6	33.5	58.6
Derbys	2.6	0.9	1.2	6.0	37.0	55.8
Leics	2.6	0.9	1.3	3.5	40.2	55.1
Lincs	5.9	0.6	10.0	1.4	22.9	65.7
Northants	2.4	0.5	1.7	0.9	34.2	63.3
Notts	2.2	1.0	1.1	11.5	29.1	58.3
North	15.4	3.1	1.3	5.5	26.0	67.1
Yorks & Humberside	15.4	4.9	1.6	5.6	27.4	65.4
East Anglia	12.6	2.0	5.4	1.3	26.5	66.8
South East	27.2	17.3	1.1	1.5	20.6	76.8
South West	23.8	4.5	3.1	1.7	24.2	70.9
West Midlands	13.0	5.2	1.5	2.4	35.8	60.3
North West	7.3	6.4	0.8	2.3	29.2	67.7
England	130.4	47.2	1.6	2.7	25.9	69.7
Wales	20.8	2.9	2.5	5.7	24.0	67.8
Scotland	77.2	5.1	1.9	3.4	22.8	71.9
N. Ireland	14.2	1.6	4.0	1.8	21.6	72.5
United Kingdom	242.5	56.8	1.7	2.9	25.4	70.0

1 – Agriculture, forestry and fishing
2 – Energy and water supply
3 – Metals, chemicals, engineering and other manufacturing
4 – Construction, distribution, transport and other services

Source: Central Statistical Office.

Given the data for the same area over several years, we can see whether it is changing in certain ways. Is its population growing? Are people moving in or out? Establishing trends is important in planning for housing, schools, etc. You can keep track of your region's trends by looking at the CSO report *Regional Trends*, which is published each year. Ask to see a copy at your local library. For example, the 1990 edition states:

> In 1988 the population of the East Midlands was just under 4 million – an increase of 3.1 per cent since 1981. This represented the third largest (regional) increase over the period . . . All the counties of the East Midlands had population increases between 1981 and 1988 with Lincolnshire at 5.4 per cent and Northamptonshire at 7.1 per cent being the largest.

However, in geography we must think very carefully about what data tell us and what they do not; that is, about data interpretation. To help us to do this we must understand other ways of getting geographical knowledge.

Images of the East Midlands – perceptions and persuaders

There are many different descriptions of places – including the East Midlands. The problem is that different people picture or perceive the same place in different ways. So in geography we must ask certain questions about descriptions of places and what is happening there. What has been included or left out? What has been pointed up or played down? Who has produced the image and why? Such information often comes from people with particular purposes and points of view. Some may want to influence our perceptions in a certain way. It is possible to illustrate this with examples from the East Midlands.

Miners' strike in the East Midlands, 1984.

D. H. Lawrence and Nottinghamshire.

During the miners' strike in 1984, there were many TV items about the large coalfield which runs through the region into South Yorkshire. Many of these images were of conflict and violence. However, much had been written about the coalfield long before the miners' strike. Compare the two very vivid but different written images of this area that are presented below.

The novels of D. H. Lawrence are world famous, and seven were set in and around the coalfield. Perhaps the most well known, *Lady Chatterley's Lover*, was banned in Britain for several years. Lawrence's views on sex were ahead of his time. However, this book also describes the coalfield area. Like Lawrence's *Sons and Lovers*, it was based on his own life around Eastwood where his father was a miner. This is how Lawrence described 'the country of my heart' in 1928, just before he died aged 44.

> I was born nearly forty-four years ago in Eastwood, a mining village of some three thousand souls about eight miles from Nottingham, and one mile from the small stream, the Erewash, which divides Nottinghamshire from Derbyshire. It is hilly country, looking west to Crich and towards Matlock, and east and north-east towards Mansfield and the Sherwood Forest. To me it seemed, and still seems an extremely beautiful countryside, just between the red sandstone and the oak trees of Nottingham, and the cold limestone, the ash trees, the stone fences of Derbyshire. To me as a child and as a young man, it was still the old England of the forest and the agricultural past; there were no motor cars, the mines were, in a sense, an accident in the landscape, and Robin Hood and his merry men were not very far away . . .
>
> D. H. Lawrence, 'Nottingham and the Mining Country', first published 1930

Now read another word-picture of the same area. The passage describes the same part of the region seen a little later, and from a different point of view. The locations are the same, even the geological features. Yet they give us totally different images of the coalfield area:

> Immediately to the west of the magnesian limestone belt, between this and the gritstone of Derbyshire, is a wide belt of Coal Measures. These begin outside Nottingham and run right away up into Western Yorkshire, the largest coalfield in Britain . . . The whole . . . is heavily industrialised. Coal has been mined here for several centuries and here other heavy industries have planted themselves – notably iron and steel works. It is a landscape of blackened grass, of stagnant pools of dirty water, and huge tips with wisps of steam rising from their steep sides. Rows of railway trucks stand disconsolately on every skyline, houses are sprinkled everywhere, short rows of them running in all directions, giving a completely planless human scene, so formless that it gives the impression at first sight of being rather in process of demolition, as if some large continuous mass had already been half destroyed.
>
> W. G. Hoskins, *East Midlands and the Peak*, 1951

Write a few sentences and/or draw sketches to show what you feel about the area after reading (a) Lawrence the novelist, and (b) Hoskins the landscape historian. List the words and phrases that most influenced your perceptions.

Recording geographical patterns: Night flight, bright lights

For centuries, getting geographical knowledge was very difficult. Images of the earth's surface were limited to rough maps and sketches. Then came the camera to give an exact image of place, and soon there were aerial photographs – the bird's-eye view became a part of geography. Better cameras and aircraft transformed map-making. **Cartography** became a science. Now the space age is bringing a whole new range of tools to geography. Satellites constantly orbit the earth and there is the new science of **remote sensing**. Computers linked to satellites can produce coloured Landsat images of the whole of the earth every few days.

While it is not yet possible to book a satellite trip across the East Midlands, we can have a bird's-eye view of some of it. Perhaps you have taken a package holiday from the East Midlands Airport. RAF pilots have been learning to fly over the region for a long time. Their most famous training base, the Royal Air Force College at Cranwell, is in Lincolnshire. Here, Instructor John Mann takes us high above the region's bright lights to describe the night-time patterns (see Fig. 1.6).

cartography
The art and science of making maps and charts from ground and aerial surveys.

remote sensing
Collecting mass data or information about objects without touching them. Data are collected scientifically by electronic devices in planes and satellites. Landsat satellites have been launched by the American space agency NASA since 1972 to map the earth's surface. Landsat 3 covers every point on earth once in every 18 days.

Flight over RAF Cranwell.

It is a clear, still night and very chilly outside – minus 13°C! Hardly surprising, because we are at 15,000 feet above the Humber estuary in our Jet Provost trainer. We are turning for base – RAF Cranwell, south of Lincoln. Coffee in the crewroom in about 20 minutes.

Tonight's sortie has been routine: out over Spalding, clipping The Wash and north up to Skegness. We turned inland on a bearing of 320°. Our second turn took us west, and our third was left again to start the descent to Cranwell. Visibility is perfect. The panel lights are dimmed and through the canopy I can see almost the whole of the East Midlands.

The coast is behind me. Ahead to my right, bearing 270°, is a big chain of lights – the Don Valley in South Yorkshire. Left of Sheffield is a long corridor of lights. It stretches for 90 kilometres to Leicester. Its brightest lights are now dead ahead on 225°. The big glow from Nottingham and Derby shows for nearly a hundred kilometres.

Out left there is even a pool of light from Peterborough beyond the dark fens and out of our region. A bit higher and we would see one from

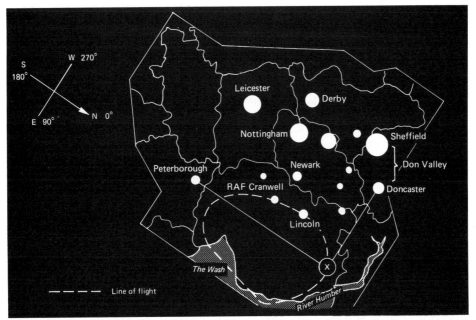

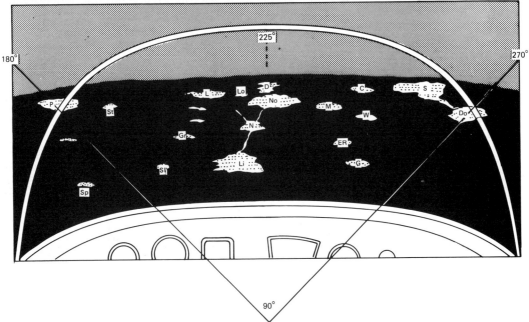

Fig. 1.6. *RAF night-flight plan and view.*

Northampton and Kettering. Down now to 5,000 feet and the straight line of street lights from Lincoln to Newark marks the Fosse Way. Don't be deceived by this detail under the Provost's nose. These Lincolnshire towns might look big places at night from here, but they are really little pools of light in a big, dark farming county.

---

1 Study Flight-Lieutenant Mann's view from the cockpit and his flight map (Fig. 1.6). Make a tracing of his map and use your atlas to mark on it as many of the places with 'bright lights' as you can.

2 Read his log again and discuss with your teacher the terms: 'minus 13°C'; 'bearing 270°'; 'Don Valley'; 'dark fens'; 'Fosse Way'.

3 Choose an area that you have flown over or would like to see from the air on a clear night. Write your own log and/or draw a sketch from the observer's seat.

geographical distribution
A pattern on the earth's surface resulting from the way features occur in relation to each other.

random distribution
A pattern that seems to have come about by chance. In the case of places, the pattern is part way between equal spacing and clustering. The lights of the East Midlands are clustered and therefore are not a random pattern or distribution.

John Mann used his trained eyes to match up the light patterns he could see from his Provost to the main settlements of the East Midlands. He was describing a **geographical distribution**. This pattern has not occurred by chance. It is not a **random distribution**. It has been built up by systematic, human activity over the centuries. To understand our present distributions we must investigate some of the 'pattern makers' of the past.

Summary

- The East Midlands, as an area, is not as clear in people's minds as the Lake District or Northern Ireland. Dividing the earth's surface into regions is an important aspect of geography. It is useful to think of formal and functional regions when studying the geography of a country like the United Kingdom.

- Different methods are used in geography to identify and describe a region like the East Midlands. It is important to understand the differences between these methods. Statistical data are very useful because they are collected for all the local government units in this country. Thus we can compare different areas within the region and also compare it with other regions. We can also look for trends and see how different areas are changing.

- People see the East Midlands in many different ways. The images of the region vary according to the methods used by those who make them. Different images of place are produced for different purposes. It is important to understand how and why different images of place are produced.

- We now have the technology to see and record patterns over the whole of areas such as the East Midlands. Geography and history help us to understand how these patterns have been formed. We need to know something of the past if we are to make sense of today's geography of the East Midlands.

2 People and places – past and present

In geography we often talk about 'natural features', meaning hills, valleys, rivers, vegetation, and so on. The patterns formed by these features are studied in physical geography. The ways in which natural features are changed by people are investigated in human geography. Almost all of the surface of the East Midlands has been altered by human activities over thousands of years. It is useful to think of the results as the **cultural landscape**.

cultural landscape
A part of the earth's surface after it has been altered by human effort.

The pattern of Fig. 2.1 is very like that seen by John Mann from his Jet Provost nearly 5 kilometres above Lincolnshire. This modern settlement pattern is the result of many movements of people and their decisions about where to live and work. The East Midlands can claim the site of some of the oldest known homes in Britain. Over 100,000 years ago, prehistoric people used cave dwellings to survive the Ice Age winters. Those at Cresswell Crags between Chesterfield and Worksop contain the best-known evidence of this period.

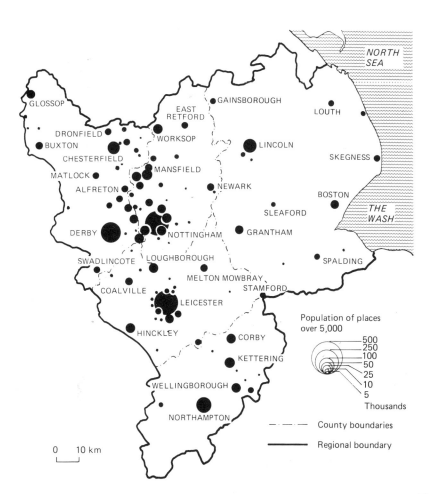

Fig. 2.1. *Settlement pattern in the East Midlands, 1975.*
Source: Based on data from the 1971 census.

Invaders and immigrants

The debris in Pin Hole Cave at Cresswell told archaeologists that people had occupied the site at least until the Romans invaded Britain, some 2,000 years ago. Today we can expect to live for about 70 years. If we divide history into 'lifetimes' of 70 years, you must think back through about 28 of them to that of Julius Caesar, who led the Romans to Britain. It is almost impossible to imagine the 1,400 'lifetimes' back to the Cresswell cave dwellers, but it reminds us how long people have been forming the region's cultural landscape. However, most of what we see today is the result of just 14 'lifetimes' – the last 1,000 years (Fig. 2.2). We can understand the region's cultural landscape better if we investigate the movements of groups of people into and across the area. These movements are well known since the Roman period.

It is important to realise how the area was perceived by tribes coming from Europe. Seen from the North Sea, the East Midlands is generally flat with several broad rivers like the Nene and the Welland flowing gently to the sea. Angles and Saxons looking for farmland and raiders like the Danes and Norsemen could easily sail up the rivers. Winters here were milder than those on the Continent, and the soils were often fertile. The drier chalk of the Lincolnshire Wolds and the limestone uplands of Leicestershire and Northamptonshire

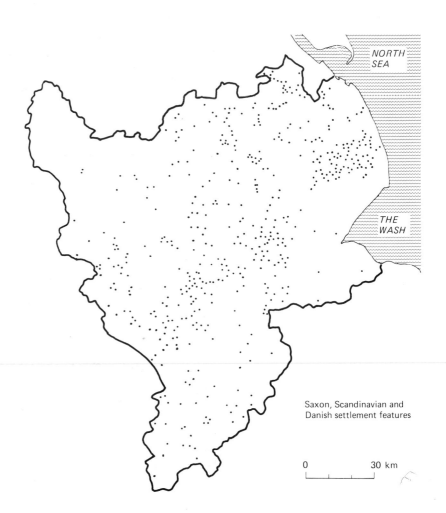

Fig. 2.2. *Settlement pattern in the East Midlands, AD 975.*
Source: Based on Ordnance Survey, *Britain before the Norman Conquest*.

were easily cleared of their trees. Therefore much of the region was an attractive environment for incoming peoples.

Each incoming group left marks on the region. The most obvious of these are the places where they chose to settle. The Romans built forts and centres of government linked by a network of good, all-weather roads. There were important Roman centres at what are now Lincoln and Leicester. The Roman fort at Lincoln was established in AD 48, and was called Lindon. As the frontier was pushed northwards, Lindon became a *colonia* – a town where retired soldiers could marry and settle. Its name changed to Lindum Colonia. Over the years this was shortened to Lincoln.

Investigating the names of places is important in human geography (Table 2.1). As in Lincoln's case, the name often indicates the origin and growth of a settlement. Place-name patterns tell us much about the development of the cultural landscape.

Table 2.1 *East Midlands – principal place-name endings*

Roman period: *AD 43–476*	
caster, cester, chester	fort or defended town
port	harbour or gate
street	paved road
Anglo-Saxon or Old English (OE) period: *circa AD 450–1100*	
First phase of settlement	
ham, ing	territory or homestead of the people of . . .
Second phase	
borough, bury	fortified settlement
bridge	bridge
ford	crossing place
ton	enclosure of land
Later clearing, drainage and establishing of smaller, linked or daughter settlements	
cot, cote	outlying hut
delph	ditch
den	pig-grazing area in wood
eg, en, eu, ey	island in marsh
fen	wet place
field	clearing in wood
hirst, hurst	copse or wooded height
holt	wood
ley	clearing
mere	lake
stoc, stoke	daughter settlement
stow	holy place
wich, wick, wike	outlying hut or dairy farm
Scandinavian period: *circa AD 800–1100*	
beck, slack	stream
booth	centre for summer pasture
by	settlement or homestead
gate	road
thorp(e)	daughter settlement
thwaite	clearing
toft	homestead

> 1 Find out all you can about the Romans, Angles, Saxons, Danes, Norsemen and Normans in your area.
> 2 Write a message from an imaginary leader of any of these groups to relatives in Europe describing your first journey across the East Midlands.
> 3 Make a list of the factors that help to explain the differences between the settlement patterns of AD 975 and 1975. (See Figs 2.1 and 2.2.)
> 4 Using Table 2.1 and a 1:50,000 Ordnance Survey (OS) map, make a list of any possible place-name evidence about invaders and immigrants in your area. Your teacher will tell you about local place-name dictionaries.

ethnic minority
A sub-group within a society that has a distinct culture of its own. Members are drawn together in various ways – by race, language, common outlook and religion.

push-pull model
An attempt to explain migration by simplifying its causes into two major sets of factors: *push* factors influence people to leave areas; *pull* factors attract to the new area.

Push-pull and permits

During the last 40 years many people from Britain's former colonies in the Caribbean, South Asia and East Africa have settled in this country. They live mainly in London and the larger towns and cities, including those of the East Midlands. Because they have distinct physical features like skin colour and their own cultures – language, dialect, religion, dress, food, music, etc. – they form important **ethnic minorities**. When trying to explain such migrations, geographers often use the **push-pull model**. This is illustrated by Fig. 2.3 in relation to immigrants from Asia.

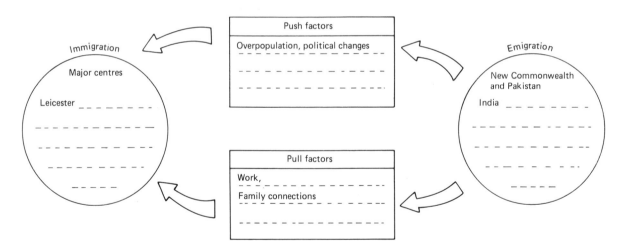

Fig. 2.3. *Push-pull model: recent immigration to the East Midlands.*

Data about the region's ethnic minorities are limited because, until 1991, the British census has not asked individuals about their ethnic group. However, it does record each person's place of birth. From this we know that in 1981 5 per cent of people then living in the East Midlands were born in other countries. Seven per cent were living in households in which the head of the household was born abroad. Table 2.2 lists the main countries or areas from which they came. Figure 2.4 shows that these most recent immigrants are concentrated in certain towns and cities and form four major groups.

Because these areas often have difficult social problems and vivid media images, it is important in geography to examine the limited data very carefully. For example, it is not always known that people from the Republic of Ireland form the second largest immigrant group in the East Midlands. They are not distinguished by colour or dress

Table 2.2 *East Midlands – origins of ethnic minorities, 1981* (persons by place of birth of head of household)

	India		East Africa		Caribbean		Pakistan		Ireland	
	No.	%	No.	%	No.	%	No.	%	No.	%
Derbyshire	9,760	15.7	690	3.1	5,040	17.7	4,087	34.3	9,940	19.6
Derby	8,320	13.4	270	1.2	1,010	3.5	3,828	32.2	4,874	
Leics.	39,800	64.1	18,040	80.6	5,880	20.7	1,783	15.0	11,466	
Leicester	34,510	55.6	15,590	69.7	5,000	17.5	1,457	12.3	6,590	22.6
Charnwood	2,900	4.7	1,210	5.4	240	0.8	115	1.0	1,300	
Lincs.	1,360	2.2	370	1.7	490	1.7	191	1.6	4,902	9.7
Northants.	4,540	7.3	2,010	9.0	5,000	17.6	573	4.8	11,947	
Northampton	1,440	2.3	720	3.2	2,940	10.2	333	2.8	5,587	23.6
Wellingboro'	1,630	2.6	860	3.7	1,560	5.5	78	0.7	1,044	
Notts.	6,620	10.7	1,260	5.6	12,050	42.3	5,272	44.3	12,392	24.5
Nottingham	4,060	6.5	640	2.9	10,100	35.5	4,828	40.6	5,894	
E. Midlands	62,080	100.0	22,370	100.0	28,460	100.0	11,906	100.0	50,647	100.0

Source: Central Statistical Office.

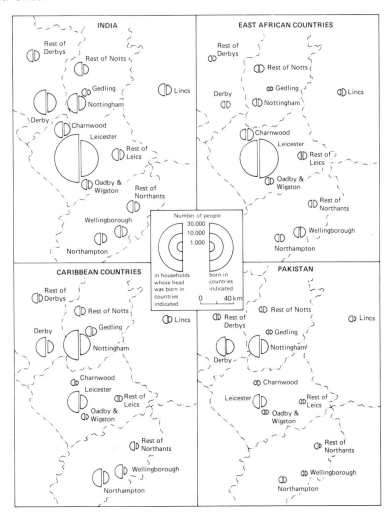

Fig. 2.4. *Distribution of ethnic minorities in the East Midlands, 1981. Source: Trent Geographer,* **5**, 1983.

Immigration Acts

Until 1962 citizens from Commonwealth countries – about one-quarter of the world's population – could settle freely in the UK. After 1962 rights of entry and settlement began to be limited by law. In 1971 an Immigration Act produced a single system of control. The British Nationality Act of 1981 restricted automatic right of settlement in the UK to Commonwealth citizens with a parent who was a UK citizen by birth, living in this country. There are no restrictions of entry or residence on people from the 'Common Travel Area' which includes the UK and the Republic of Ireland.

and they are more widely scattered. While the 1971 **Immigration Act** restricts the number of people from the four groups shown in Fig. 2.4 coming into Britain, the Irish can enter Britain more freely. So migration has important economic and political results. When using simple models of migration we must remember that the reality of human movement is very complex. Individuals and families in some ethnic groups are greatly affected by laws controlling migration. In geography we must try to understand different people's perceptions of migration and its results in areas like the East Midlands. In the following extract, Irving and Verit Mayers, who came to England from Barbados in 1962, look back on their experiences:

'The West Indies didn't offer much when you left school at 14 in the '50s,' recalled Irving. 'You hadn't many chances with only three bursaries among all the kids in St Joseph's parish. The rest just couldn't afford to stay on and study for certificates or apprenticeships. It was five years before I got lucky with a government job in the Soil Survey. My, it was a lot better than working on the land. I had "green fingers" all right but they didn't earn me much!

'When I began talking about emigrating, the Senior Surveyor warned me to beware. He was English and a fine man in every way. So why didn't I listen? Well, the British Transport Commission was offering guaranteed jobs and lending the boat fare to England. You didn't know where you would be sent but it was all the rage with radio adverts and mobile cinemas going round the villages. I reckon I was "pulled" by it all and my mates signing up. You wanted to prove you could do it too. Then there was my dad. He had worked a lot of farm contracts in Florida and was respected for it. That gave a bit of "push"!

'Anyway, I came ashore on 6th March 1962 and was sent straight up to Nottingham. Four of us lads from Barbados lived in the old Meadows. My, was it damp! They walked to work at the Midland Station but I had to bus it out to Toton Sidings. Being a shed-man wasn't what I had imagined but I thought I'd work a three-year contract and then go back home with a bank balance.'

'No way,' laughed Vee. 'It's more like eight contracts and he's still at Toton!'

'Well, I found a wife,' retorted Irving.

'True, we met at a cousin's wedding in 1963. I was up from London. I'd come over to try to make better money as a seamstress in Islington where I had relatives,' remembered Vee. 'They were "pulling" and my mother was "pushing" because I wasn't always paid properly by people whose clothes I'd made back home. Well, I've done all sorts of work here but not earned much real money. That's partly down to the low wages women seem to get in Nottingham for my sort of work, but sometimes it's been sheer prejudice. Oh, I'd go back tomorrow but it's not as simple as that. Irving's kept his job. A lot who came with us haven't, and we've got our family here. We've had to move house a lot – usually because of damp, which has made me ill. Also we like a bit of peace, which is why we left Hyson Green flats. Looking back, we just didn't know enough when we emigrated. But now we have our lovely grand-daughter just round the corner. Look at all those photos on the walls! She's a joy and we can see her any day.'

---

1 Copy Fig. 2.3, and fill in the spaces.
2 Write a short history of your family and its movements since 1960. Compare it with the Mayers' family story.

core-periphery model
This tries to explain major contrasts in economic development between central and outer areas in a country or region.

conurbation
A term first used by planners to describe large, continuously built-up areas where once-separate settlements have grown into each other, for example Greater London, and the West Midlands.

Cores, peripheries and corridors

The **core-periphery model** is another way of trying to simplify and understand complicated distributions of people. Again a simple diagram (Fig. 2.5) illustrates the basic idea of a crowded central area or 'core' surrounded by a larger area with fewer people, jobs and services (see Table 2.3). Many regions have population patterns that fit this model, including the West Midlands with its **conurbation** based on Birmingham.

In the East Midlands there is a marked concentration of population in the Leicester–Derby–Nottingham area. There is also an extension northwards to Mansfield and Alfreton. The area is not classed as a conurbation but there are some core-periphery features. There is a steep population gradient eastwards to north-east Leicestershire and Lincolnshire.

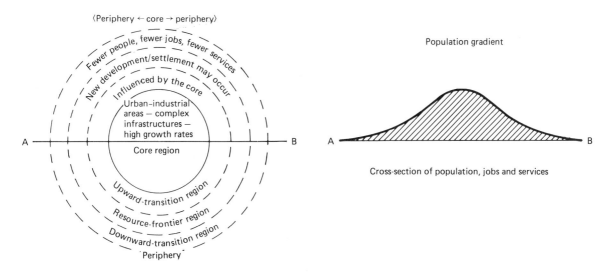

Fig. 2.5. *Core-periphery model.*

> Choose any area you know or have studied that shows core-periphery features.
> 1 Construct a table based on Table 2.3 to show these features, adding a section on 'Health and welfare'.
> 2 Draw up a balance sheet headed 'The Quality of Life', to show your own preference for living in a core or periphery area.

cumulative causation
A theory to explain increases in economic differences between areas in terms of multiplier or 'knock-on' effects. For example, the growth of a new industry brings new jobs followed by extra spending by the workers and demand for new services and products, leading to more employment, and so on.

The reasons for these concentrations or cores of people, work and services are not simple. To try to explain them, geographers use the idea of **cumulative causation**. The growth of a core is compared to that of a rolling snowball or the pull of a magnet. Figure 2.6 shows how this 'knock-on' effect is believed to operate. If we investigate population changes in the region during the 1980s, another pattern begins to appear. Table 2.4 shows that population growth was almost twice the average for England and Wales. Figure 2.7 gives more detail on these changes at the district level.

Thus we can detect a sort of 'corridor of growth' extending into the region from the south. It stretches from Northampton through Leicestershire to Derby and Nottingham. However, the cities themselves are exceptions. In the period 1981–85, Derby, Leicester and Nottingham all lost population. By contrast, Northampton recorded the region's largest increase: 17 per cent.

Table 2.3 *Core-periphery analysis – a comparison of Nottingham and Boston District*

	Greater Nottingham*	**Boston District**
Population	567,000 (1981)	52,000 (1981)
Settlement	High density Wide range of dwelling types House prices higher Large council estates High-rise housing areas Wide range of private rented accommodation including sub-standard inner-city housing	Lower density Limited range of dwelling types House prices lower Smaller areas of council housing No high-rise housing Smaller range of private rented accommodation including houses 'tied' to farm jobs; less sub-standard property
Work	Wide range of industrial and service jobs Higher average earnings Lower average unemployment Large-scale industries, e.g. Boots, Plessey Considerable government- generated work, e.g. Civil Service, Aspley, Royal Ordnance Factory, Meadows	Narrower range of jobs, many on farms or related to agriculture Lower average earnings Higher average unemployment Smaller-scale industries, mainly in Boston Little government-generated employment
Services	All basic services throughout area Wide range of retailing, several supermarkets and superstores Several large hotels and conference centres Large office blocks County and city halls Polytechnic, university, five colleges of further education Large central library Three large hospitals and medical school Two professional theatres Several multi-screen cinemas Two large concert halls Two football league clubs, county and test cricket Inter-city rail and two major bus stations	Not all services everywhere, e.g. town gas and mains drainage Smaller range, fewer supermarkets, no shopping malls or superstores No large hotels or conference facilities Small private offices only Small civic centre buildings No higher education facilities; one college of further education No large library facility One medium-sized modern hospital No permanent professional theatre Limited cinema services No major concert hall No football league clubs, county cricket Provincial rail links only, local bus services only

* City of Nottingham, Broxtowe, Gedling, Rushcliffe

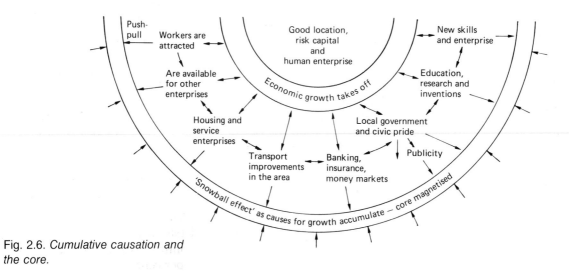

Fig. 2.6. *Cumulative causation and the core.*

Table 2.4 *Population changes in the East Midlands, 1971–85*

County	Intercensal change 1971–81, average rate % per year	Mid-year population (thousands) 1981	1985	Change 1981–85, average rate % per year
Derbyshire	2.66	914.4	912.4	−0.5
Leicestershire	5.62	858.8	872.2	4.0
Lincolnshire	9.39	552.6	560.3	3.5
Northamptonshire	12.77	532.6	546.1	6.25
Nottinghamshire	1.10	994.3	995.5	0.3
East Midlands	5.13	3,852.7	3,896.9	2.75
England and Wales	0.83	49,634.3	49,923.5	1.5

Source: Central Statistical Office.

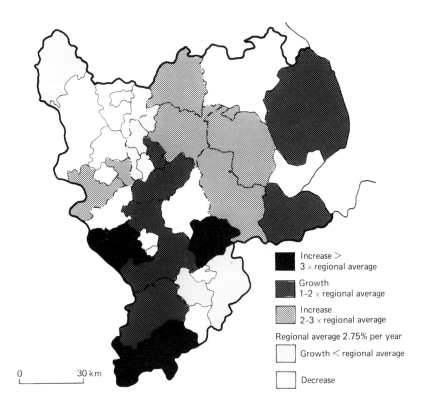

Fig. 2.7. *Population change in the East Midlands by district*, 1981–85. Source: *Trent Geographer*, **9–10**, 1986.

demography
The study of population data.

natural change
Changes in population due to the differences between births and deaths in the area.

Such trends in the region's **demography** may be a result of either **natural change** or migration. Births exceeded deaths throughout most of the East Midlands from 1971 to 1981, and again up to 1985. Some of the peripheral areas in Derbyshire and Lincolnshire recorded a natural decrease, but the pattern seen in Figure 2.7 is largely a result of people moving.

In this chapter we have learned that such movements have been typical of the region's history. Later, in Chapter 8, we will investigate population flows that are continuing, and the reasons for them.

Summary

- The pattern of settlement in the East Midlands today is the outcome of many decisions made by people in the past about where to live and work.
- We can understand this pattern better if we know about important movements or migrations across and within what is now called the East Midlands.
- It is also important to consider recent immigration into the region, the factors influencing it and its effect on settlement and social patterns.
- We can think too of the region's settlements as forming economic cores, which attract population, jobs and services, and as peripheries, where these are fewer. In the East Midlands in the 1990s there is evidence of a corridor rather than a core of economic growth.
- Cumulative causation helps to explain concentrations of economic activity and growth in the region.

3 Rocks, rivers and resources

> From west to east the East Midlands region is just about a hundred miles across. It runs from the great Pennine watershed of England to the North Sea . . . it contains every type of English scenery to some degree.
> W. G. Hoskins, *East Midlands and the Peak*, 1951

Between the High Peak and the Fens, rocks and landscapes change in rapid succession. Grits, limestones, Coal Measures, red sandstones, clay and chalk appear like ribs on a west–east section. Further south, Matlock's minerals and springs are a reminder of volcanoes long extinct. The dark rocks of Charnwood Forest are among the oldest in Britain. See Fig. 3.1.

The region's rivers have cut through this rich variety of geology to add to the landscape patterns. The Trent, one of England's major rivers, dominates the north and west of the area. Its tributaries, the Dove and the Derwent, feed melting snow and rain from the Peak District through their famous dales and gorges. The Trent Basin is part of the large water resource system controlled by the former Severn–Trent Water Authority, now a private company. In the south and east, the Nene, Welland and Witham drain a gentler landscape to the Wash. These rivers are also linked into another vital **hydrological system** by the former Anglian Water Authority. Every aspect of the region's life depends to some extent on these water resources. The water authorities added to the region's physical variety by creating great storage lakes like the Derwent Reservoirs and Rutland Water.

Figure 3.1 shows the basic features of the region's physical structure. We can see the general distribution of the rocks and rivers, but what is this varied landscape really like? What do you see when you cross the East Midlands?

hydrological system
Hydrology is the study of water on or near the earth's surface. Hydrological systems link all the movements of water between the atmosphere, the oceans and the land. (See Chapter 6 for systems in geography.)

Low flights – insights

'What you see depends upon where you are and what you are looking for,' says Paul Murray, a student pilot at RAF Cranwell. '250 feet in daylight is very different from 15,000 feet at night!' Here Paul gives a detailed account of a low-level sortie across the region with his instructor, Flight-Lieutenant Steve Biglands. This was Paul's introduction to the strict discipline of low-level missions and he had some high-speed map reading to do.

> We dropped to a low level above the radio beacon near Ruskington. Steve switched onto it to get checks for our timing and turning points, but really you quickly have to match what you see below with what is on your map. It's a special edition showing power lines and other obstacles. There are plenty in the Trent Valley. It's a huge power house!
>
> Heading west towards the Lincoln Edge the soil was rich brown. The stone villages and farms looked neat and tidy. I felt I could touch the tall church steeples just beyond our wing-tips. We seemed to soar as the

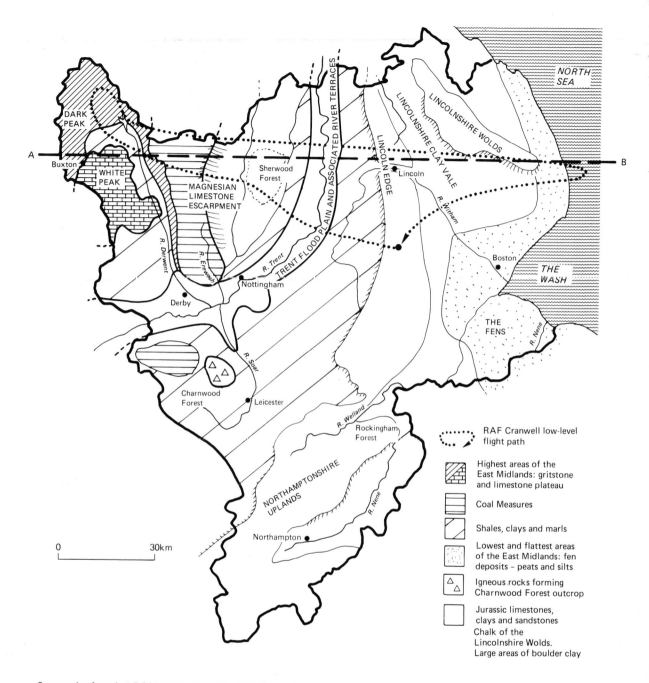

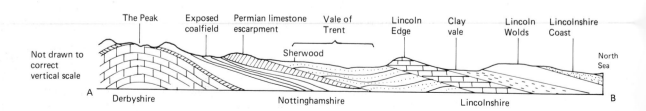

Fig. 3.1. *Physical geography of the East Midlands.*

River Trent, near Muskham.

Provost cleared the Edge. From the right-hand seat I saw a line of villages stretching north towards Lincoln. I got my first chance with the camera when we entered the Trent Valley. Remember, everything is much closer than it looks on the photographs. You don't have a lot of time at five miles a minute! You can't mistake the Trent, though, with its meanders, locks, barges and, always in view, big power stations. We were soon across it and over the great blocks of conifers that make up most of Sherwood Forest today. But we had some good markers with headgear sticking up from big mining villages like Ollerton.

Then came a big change. Steve climbed to the regulation 2,000 feet for urban areas. Houses, roads, rail sidings, mines, factories, tips and quarries were everywhere – the old coalfield. But it's not all ugly. Bolsover Castle seemed very grand on its crag looking down on the M1. The motorway is a perfect marker for the pilot but just here it's frightening to see a huge opencast pit being worked right beside the six lanes packed with vehicles.

Bolsover Castle.

M1 near Markham.

Hope Valley cement works.

Derwent reservoirs.

We stayed at 2,000 feet over Chesterfield. Then we dropped again to a low level and Steve soon had to lift the nose over rising ground and some small dams. The green fields with dark, stone walls suddenly gave way to empty, brown moor. We passed close to massive, dark rock edges facing west. Then, just as quickly, we were into a green valley. I spotted Baslow around its bridge over the Derwent. Steve turned sharply to follow the river upstream. More huge rock faces on my right meant Froggart Edge. We were suddenly level with the bright red ropes of some climbers. Then we were into a wider valley. We turned gently round our marker – the tall chimney of the Hope Valley cement works. This looked out of place among the neat, white-walled fields in the National Park, but was soon behind us. We began to climb over the edge of Kinder Scout, the highest and most westerly point on our flight plan. We were skimming a real wilderness compared with the Hope Valley: black peat bog half-covered in snow – it seemed flat and featureless.

It's easy to get lost up there, and we both looked hard for the Snake Pass road and the Derwent Reservoirs. Steve saw them first. My inside really suffered when he put the nose down in a turn. He'd decided to follow a route that took us only just over the long, dark lakes and huge, white walls. I knew there were houses and a church under that black water, which seemed to go on for ever as we twisted and turned along the flooded valleys. Relief for me as we climbed again and turned to avoid Sheffield. We headed east at 4,000 feet and the Pennines were soon behind. On my side the low winter sun picked out the Trent meanders again.

Flood plain of the River Trent.

Worksop, East Retford, Lincoln and Horncastle were easy markers from that height, but the cathedral and the Witham Gap didn't stand out in the way I had expected. The Lincolnshire Wolds weren't too obvious either until we dropped down to low level again and I realised how big the fields were with chalk pits and storage ponds.

Chapel St Leonards.

There was no mistaking the holiday coast as we left the flat pastures and lifted over the sand dunes. From that height they seemed to me higher than the Wolds. There was a whole town of caravans as we turned tightly around the beach and groynes. We were on the last leg west back to base. The Wolds again, a wooded area near Woodhall Spa, and then the Fens were passing just below the nose like a giant's chessboard.

River Witham, and Lincoln Cathedral in the far distance.

I realised that the gleaming zig-zag cutting across the squares was the Witham with its straightened, built-up banks. The sugar beet factory at Bardney was our final marker. Now on the northern horizon we really could see Lincoln Cathedral perched above the river gap. An hour after take-off we were back over the tower.

> 1 Plot Paul's flight path on a large-scale map of the area.
> 2 Using the photographs and his description, try to divide his route into formal regions.
> 3 Produce your own illustrated account of a low-level flight over an area you know well.

Dark Peak, White Peak

When Paul flew over north Derbyshire he saw 'dark rock edges' and 'black peat bog'. He also noted the 'white-walled fields' near the Hope Valley cement works. These features reflect two distinct landscapes which make up most of the **Peak National Park**. These areas are valued and protected partly for the splendid scenery which attracts millions of visitors, and partly because the particular combinations of rocks, climate, vegetation and wildlife produce distinct **ecosystems** (Fig. 3.2).

Fig. 3.2. *The White Peak and the Dark Peak.*
Source: Based on *Peak Park Structure Plan 1974.*

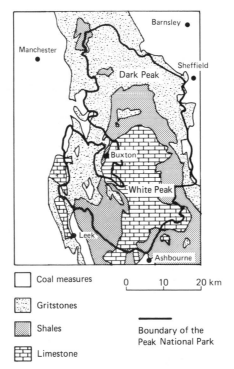

The White Peak

Limestone is a very permeable rock with many joints and cracks through which rainwater easily passes. This water is slightly acid and slowly dissolves the rock to form underground caves and pot holes.

The White Peak is made of limestone that was formed about 330 million years ago from the remains of sea creatures which collected on the bed of the shallow, tropical sea which once covered most of northern England.

Limestone wildlife

The soil of the limestone plateau is fertile and supports a great variety of wildlife. The dales are sometimes wooded, mainly with Ash.

White-flowered Spring Sandwort is locally known as Leadwort because it is one of the few plants that will grow on the spoil heaps left by lead miners.

The Dark Peak

The Peakland Edges
Where the gritstone cap was eroded and the limestone is first revealed, long walls of rock called 'edges' are left, overlooking the river valleys far below.

These gritstone edges run for several miles down both eastern and western sides of the Peak National Park. They provide good views and are the favourite places of rock climbers. Stream and river valleys in gritstone country are called 'cloughs' and often support old oak woods. (What was gritstone used for?)

In contrast to the limestone, the Dark Peak creates very acid soil conditions. Few plants can survive, but one that does and enjoys the wet is the fluffy, white-headed Cotton Grass.

Heather also likes acid soils and covers many parts of the better-drained moors. It is regularly burnt and 'managed' to support the Red Grouse.

Peak National Park

Formerly the Peak District National Park, the first of ten beautiful and relatively wild areas in England and Wales to be protected under the 1949 National Parks and Access to the Countryside Act. The others, by age, are the Lake District, Snowdonia, Dartmoor, Pembrokeshire Coast, North Yorkshire Moors, Yorkshire Dales, Exmoor, Northumberland and the Brecon Beacons National Parks.

ecosystem

Grouping of certain types of plants and animals linked by a particular environment. The ways in which the elements of an ecosystem are held together are very complex and need careful study.

The Dark Peak gets its name from the sombre colour of peat moors, rock edges and stone walls. Here there are really two environments – the moorlands and the valleys. The moorlands are both on the grit edges and on the high plateaus. The vegetation is largely heather, bilberry and cotton grass, often growing on deep peat deposits. In the valleys it gives way to bracken and rough pasture, and in the valley bottoms there are trees, bushes and walled fields of improved pasture.

The White Peak is a result of ecosystems based on the limestone uplands and dales. Again there are two landscapes. The upland plateaus are mainly improved pasture within small, walled fields. There are clumps and belts of beech, ash and sycamore but the shorter grasses, grey-white walls and rock outcrops combine to give a much lighter landscape. The plant and animal communities are very different from those of the Dark Peak. There are distinct types of grasses, clovers and buttercups. Often they are so well adapted to their ecosystem that they produce good meadows year after year without modern farming methods.

1 Using a suitable atlas, mark and name the country's national parks on a map of Britain.
2 Make a table listing their main features and any distinctive ecologies they may protect.
3 Use words and sketches to describe any ecosystem that you know at first hand.

Dams, dykes and defences

Complex hydrological systems to use the water cycle have been developed in the region over many years. Almost every part of the East Midlands now receives clean water from a network of reservoirs, pumping stations, treatment plants and pipes. Because much of the Lincolnshire coast is low lying and at risk from high tides and winds, there is also a system of water defences. None of this is cheap.

East Coast floods, 1953.

public sector
This is the part of a country's economy owned and controlled by government. It includes all the departments of central and local government and nationalised industries. The basic purpose of the public sector is to ensure the welfare of the whole community rather than make a profit for shareholders, which is the purpose of the private sector of the economy. (See Chapter 4 for nationalisation.)

privatisation
Since 1979 one of the main aims of Conservative governments has been to reduce the size of the public sector. This has been done both by selling public enterprises like British Airways and by contracting out to private firms former public work, e.g. refuse collection. These methods of extending the private sector are known as privatisation.

Paying the bills – public or private?

By the 1960s it was realised that demand for water services could easily double in Britain by the year 2000. Hundreds of authorities, public and private, were then involved in modifying the water cycle. Parliament decided that this was wasteful and not the best way of planning for future demand. So in 1973 a Water Act created ten large water authorities based on river basins and responsible for all water resources. Until 1989 these authorities were in the **public sector**. Their costs were met by water charges which all property owners paid by law. By the late 1980s there were sharply conflicting political views on water supply. The Conservative government intended to **privatise** the water authorities, and did so in 1989. The opposition parties remained in favour of public ownership. The situation is complicated by the wide range of geographical conditions under which water suppliers must operate. Some of these are seen in the East Midlands (Fig. 3.3).

Anglian Water is the largest regional water authority in England and Wales in terms of area covered.

The flat terrain and scattered population create a number of major operational and planning problems for Anglian Water, all of which add to the costs of providing the essential services of water supply, sewerage and sewage treatment, land drainage and sea defences.

The facts:

- The region is the driest part of the country. Effective rainfall is less than a third of the national average, and this makes the task of collecting and conserving water more difficult and costly.

- Rivers are a major water resource. In this area they are slow moving, and pollution has a greater impact. Their extensive use demands high standards of treatment and control over the discharge of effluent.

- About 20 per cent of the region is below sea level and it has the longest and most vulnerable coastline. The costs of keeping the largest agricultural area in England dry and drained are high.

- All clean and dirty water has to be pumped, often over long distances. Power costs, particularly of electricity, are a substantial slice of Anglian's operating costs.

- More small pumping stations have to be provided to move water to and from customers.

- Scattered communities and a low population density require more and longer pipe runs – the sewers and water mains in Anglian are a third longer than the national average – and more small sewage works are needed, which are costly to run. More than 85 per cent of works serve populations of less than 5,000.

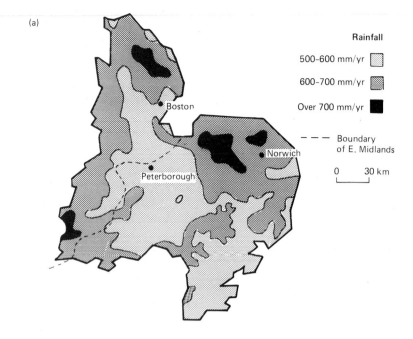

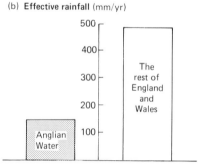

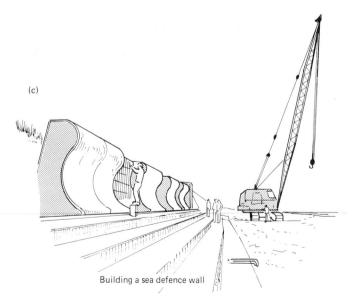

Building a sea defence wall

As with a river system, a coastline, if left to its own devices, will change its shape. The changes that can occur as a result of wave action may, in the event of a major storm, be far more dramatic than the results of river bank erosion. Where the action of the sea simply results in erosion and loss of land, engineering work is carried out to prevent this, usually by the District Council. However, where the land behind the coastline is low-lying and the action of the sea is likely to breach the coastline under high tidal surge conditions and cause flooding, then costly engineering designed to prevent such flooding is generally the responsibility of the Water Authority. The defences may take the form of natural sand dunes and shingle ridges, or artificial embankments and walls made from concrete or steel sheet piling.

Fig. 3.3. *Anglian Water – the facts.*
Source: Anglian Water, 1985.

1 Write a letter from the Anglian Water Company to a customer in Lincolnshire who has complained about water charges.
2 Design a publicity sheet explaining the water services and costs in your area.
3 Draft two parliamentary speeches, one arguing for the privatisation of the water authorities, the other defending public ownership.

Inputs and outputs

The problems faced by water authorities are largely to do with balancing hydrological inputs and outputs. In Britain there is often too little water in the place where and at the time when it is needed most. Elsewhere there may be much more than can be used locally. John Pirt, a senior resources officer with Severn–Trent, tells us about this in the East Midlands (see Fig. 3.4 for its geological history).

> In Leicestershire, geology, climate and population interact to cause water resource problems. People living in Leicester and the towns along the River Soar need large quantities of clean water. Industry, agriculture and navigation add to demand. However, the rainfall here is relatively low.

Era	Period or system	Years ago (millions)	Main rock types and locations in the East Midlands	
Quaternary	Recent		Fenland silts	east coast to the Wash
			Peatland silts	R. Witham and R. Nene
			River alluvium	Trent and Welland Valleys
	Pleistocene	2	Boulder clay and drift	large areas of east and south Lincs. Leics. and Northants.
Cainozoic	Pliocene			
	Miocene			
	Oligocene			
	Eocene			
	Palaeocene	65		
Mesozoic	Cretaceous		Chalk	Lincolnshire Wolds
			Lower Cretaceous clays	Spilsby – Lincs.
		136	Clays	
	Jurassic		Oolitic limestone	Lincoln Edge
			Ironstones	Lincs. and Northants.
		183	Sandstones and clays	Belt lying east of R. Trent and R. Soar
	Rhaetic	193		
	Triassic		Keuper marl	South Derbys./north-west Leics. – middle Trent Valley, lower Derwent and Soar Valleys
		220	Bunter sandstone	Sherwood Forest–Nottingham
Palaeozoic	Permian	280	Magnesian limestone	N–S escarpment marks boundary of exposed–concealed coalfield
	Carboniferous		Coal measures	Derby–Notts. and Leics.
			Millstone grit	Dark Peak and 'The Edges'
		345	Carboniferous limestone	White Peak
	Devonian	395		
	Silurian	435		
	Ordovician	500		
	Cambrian	570		
Pre-cambrian	Pre-Cambrian		Granite-like syenite	Charnwood Forest
			Slates - metamorphic	

Fig. 3.4. *Geological time-scale of the East Midlands.*

strata
Plural of *stratum* (Latin), a layer or bed (of sedimentary rock). This is formed by the deposition of sediments – material from other rocks, or organisms, usually in water.

impermeable marl
A chalky clay which does not let water pass easily through it. Clay is porous – that is, it has pores or spaces in it. However, these pores quickly fill with water, making the clay impermeable.

surface runoff
The movement of water across the land, usually after heavy rain, which happens because the vegetation and the soil cannot intercept and absorb it quickly enough.

baseflow
The water that soaks down or infiltrates through the soil into rock strata provides a steady supply to streams and rivers. This is known as their baseflow.

regime
A stream or river flows for most of the time at a level that is well suited to its channel and surrounding land surface. This typical pattern of flow is known as its regime.

Carboniferous strata
Layers of rock that were laid down during a period of geological time in which coal-bearing rocks were formed. The Carboniferous period was roughly 280–330 million years ago and produced most of our Coal Measures. (The other main periods and their features in the East Midlands are shown in Fig. 3.4.)

groundwater
All the water occupying pores, cracks and spaces in the soil and rock strata.

Fig. 3.5. *Runoff response from 25 mm rainfall by the River Sence at Blaby and the River Wye at Ashford.**
Source: Dr John Pirt, Severn-Trent Water.

* The River Sence flows south of Leicester to join the River Soar. The River Wye flows from the Derbyshire Peak District through limestone in the Ashford area.

Much of what falls passes quickly out of the basin before we can use it. This is because the underlying **strata** are **impermeable marls** and clays. These do not easily hold or store water. When there is heavy rain these rocks produce a lot of **surface runoff**. This may cover much of the flood plain. But once the flood has gone, the strata hold little water, so that **baseflow** is low in dry months. Water supplies may be at risk.

Flooding on the River Soar.

In the Peak District we have a different **regime** and different problems. There is much more rain and snow, but lower population and demand. Here the **Carboniferous strata** form the main rocks. They are permeable, which means that more water penetrates giving lower surface runoff than on Leicestershire's impermeable clays. Also, more water is held in surface depressions and by vegetation. In effect, this **groundwater** is a reservoir. It gives us a much better baseflow, as the input eventually emerges as springs and streams. This is shown by the graphs recording runoff from the River Sence in Leicestershire and the River Wye in Derbyshire [Fig. 3.5].

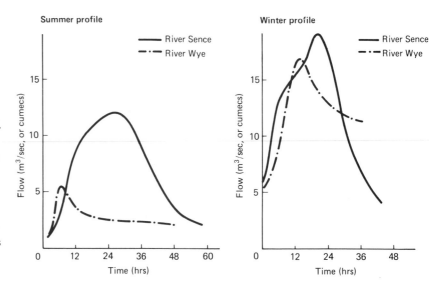

We tackle this input-output problem by moving water from the 'wet' uplands of the region to the 'dry' demand areas in the lowlands. This has been done for years. The old method was to construct large reservoirs in the areas of high precipitation and reliable baseflow like the Derwent Valleys. The water then goes by long pipelines to the demand areas. Our new system uses the region's rivers to take the water to the south. This is held at pump storage reservoirs like Church Wilne near Long Eaton. These can only be filled by pumping from the Derwent. This method can be cheaper but is difficult to engineer. The transporting watercourse must be free from pollution. This is not easy to ensure in industrial areas. We use both systems in the East Midlands, as the map shows [Fig. 3.6].

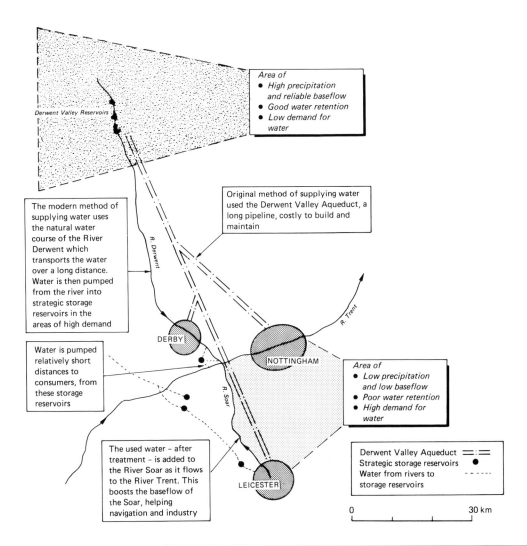

Fig. 3.6. *Severn-Trent Water Authority provision system.*
Source: Based on Severn-Trent Water Authority data.

1 Discuss the following with your teacher: geology, climate and population interact; input-output problems; transporting watercourse.
2 Compare and contrast the line graphs (Fig. 3.5) for runoff response and daily mean flow at Blaby and Ashford. Try to explain the differences.
3 Find out as much as you can about the water supply system in your area, including any water transfer system that may be used by your water company.

Summary

- The rocks, relief and drainage of the East Midlands are very varied. We can identify several different physical areas within the region. These have all been modified by human activity over long periods so that today there are various, distinct landscapes or sub-regions.
- Some of the landscapes within the East Midlands can be understood better if we study their ecosystems.
- The control and use of the rivers and the sea in the region are very important to the way of life here. In some areas the modification of the water cycle has produced new physical features and new ecosystems.
- The region's water resources were the responsibility of two water authorities which became private companies in 1989. Their work influences the lives of everyone in the East Midlands. The ownership of water resources became a major political issue in the late 1980s.

4 Rocks, riches and renewal

Figure 4.1 indicates the variety of useful rocks and minerals in the region. There is a long history of turning rocks to riches in the East Midlands. The Romans took lead and fluorspar from Derbyshire. A visit to the Lead Mining Museum at Matlock Bath will show you how a single mineral can influence the life and landscape of an area – but this only happens so long as it can be mined at a profit.

King Coal and the ironmasters

The main coalmining areas in the East Midlands are at the southern end of a great belt of Coal Measures following the eastern and southern flanks of the Pennines (see Fig. 4.1). Both coal and iron have been dug from the shallow seams of the **exposed Coal Measures** for many centuries. Small-scale ironmaking was well established by 1700 between Chesterfield and Ilkeston. The ironstone was easily mined. Charcoal came from woodlands on large estates like those of the Duke of Devonshire. Fast streams turned mill wheels and powered the bellows.

By 1750 iron ore was being imported from Europe via Boston but charcoal smelting was becoming uneconomic. The Derbyshire ironmasters turned to a new coal-based fuel, coke. This cut costs because they were often coal-owners themselves. More profits from coal came in the 1770s with the arrival of the canal age. By 1800 the new waterway system meant that Derbyshire coal and iron could be sold competitively throughout the country.

It was now obvious to the Derbyshire industrial **entrepreneurs** that transport improvements were the key to greater riches from the area's rocks. Canals were a big advance on pack horses and muddy roads, but barge transport was slow. The **cuts** or **navigations** were also limited by height and relief. Another invention was needed. The answer was the 'iron horse' on the iron rail.

By 1830 the railway age had begun and the market for Derbyshire iron expanded again. Wider markets reached by rail and lower production costs led to more expansion. By 1859 Derbyshire had 43 furnaces making 188,000 tons of pig-iron. This was ten times the output before the coming of the railways. The East Midlands was becoming an important part of a new national industrial system.

The Victorian age was one of great expansion for British industry. Markets and profits grew almost continuously as Britain built up the largest empire the world has ever seen. Before Victoria died she ruled about 45 million people in the United Kingdom, and her empire had a total population of over 400 million! It was linked by iron rails and steamships. Coal was king of the new industrial world. The East Midlands was part of it.

By 1901, when Queen Victoria died, large parts of the region were urbanised and industrialised. That is, the farmland of 1800 had been

---

exposed Coal Measures
The coal-bearing rocks of the Carboniferous period were first found and mined on or near the surface. These early mining areas in the west of the region are known as the *exposed coalfield*. Further east the Coal Measures under the younger rocks are called the *concealed coalfield*.

entrepreneur
A person who starts and organises a business, risking money to begin operations in the hope of making a profit. Entrepreneurs are particularly important in periods of economic change, as in the first industrial revolution, and in the current growth of new high-tech industries.

cut/navigation
The early names for canals constructed to carry goods. The men who dug these industrial canals, often with picks and shovels, became known as *navvies*. The word was later used for construction workers in general.

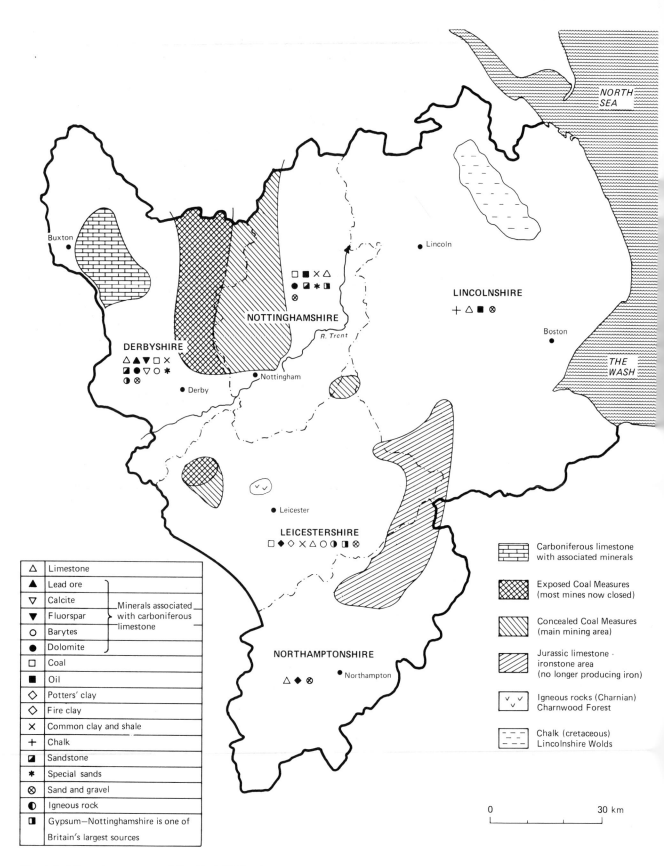

Fig. 4.1. *Mineral resources of the East Midlands.*

replaced by towns, mines, factories, quarries and tips. There was a network of railways and sidings. In East Derbyshire, industry had brought totally new settlements. There were company villages and small towns like Codnor Park and Ironville in the Erewash Valley.

In Lincolnshire and Northamptonshire, geological surveys had plotted the valuable iron ore deposits of the Jurassic strata in the south and east of the region. They were soon found to be more profitable for ironmaking. New riches were beginning to come from different rocks in the south and east of the region. Industrial locations, landscapes and lifestyles were changing again in the East Midlands. Soon a major iron and steel area was to develop in Northamptonshire (see Chapter 7).

Migrating mines

Coalmining has also moved eastwards in a clear and important way. The coal-bearing Carboniferous strata dip to the east under the newer rocks (Fig. 4.2). The coal and iron nearest to the surface were mined first. The impact was felt in east Derbyshire especially after about 1750. By 1870 there were at least 150 mines working the shallower deposits in the west of the region. However, the mines had begun to 'migrate' to the east. There were also 15 mines sunk deep into the 'concealed field' in Derbyshire and Nottinghamshire. The process has continued throughout this century (Fig. 4.3).

Costs to the communities

Great wealth has been created in the East Midlands by digging coal from the rocks, but there have been many costs. In the last century men, women and children all worked underground in Britain's coal mines. Many were killed or injured in accidents or became ill because of the working conditions.

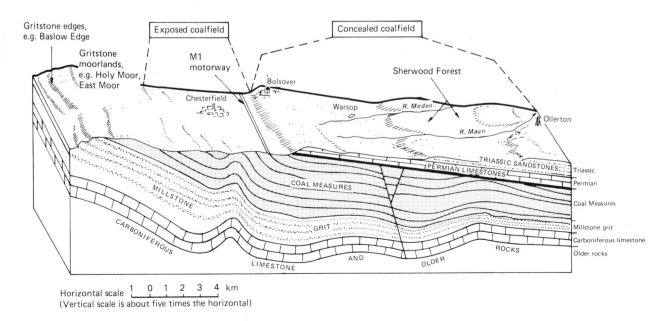

Fig. 4.2. *Structure of the Notts-Derby coalfield.*

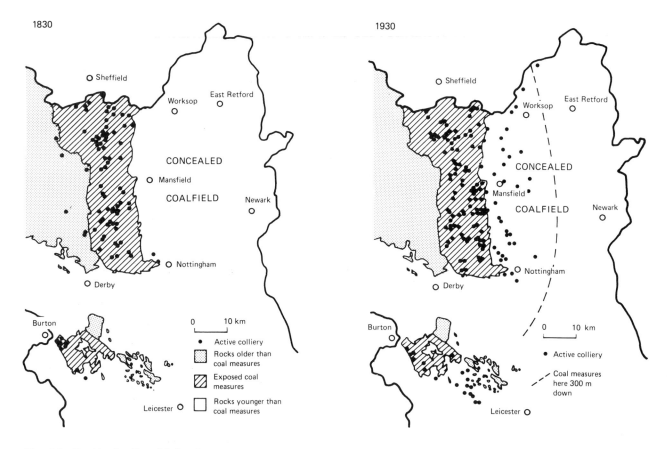

Fig. 4.3. *Coal in the East Midlands, 1830 and 1930.*
Source: Based on G. H. Dury, *The East Midlands and the Peak*, Nelson 1963.

---

nationalisation
The process of taking land, property, industries and other economic assets into the public sector or 'state ownership' with the aim of protecting national interests. Several basic industries, including coal, were nationalised by Britain's first Labour government with a large majority (1945–50). The Conservative governments' privatisation policies from 1979 onwards can be regarded as, in part, a reaction to nationalisation. It is based on the opposing view that the national interest is best served by private ownership.

Mining communities have always been strong. They are united by danger and by belonging to a particular place where coal can be worked. Coalmining is still hard and dangerous work. There were 141 fatal accidents in British coal mines between 1979 and 1989. Miners have organised some of the strongest trades unions. These supported the **nationalisation** of the coal industry in 1947.

However, by then the industry had already passed its peak production – 292 million tonnes in 1913. In the period between the two World Wars (1918–39), the industry went through depressions and strikes as the world markets for coal changed. Life was hard in mining areas, including those in the East Midlands. After the Second World War and nationalisation, employment and earnings improved greatly in the industry as world markets recovered. Production reached 217 million tonnes in 1954 but has declined since in the face of competition from oil, natural gas and nuclear fuels (Table 4.1).

Pits, power and pollution

Coal production has also fallen in the East Midlands, but not on the same scale as in some areas. Indeed, by 1980 the region was Britain's major producer, with about one-third of national output. Coal remains Britain's major source of energy in the late 1980s. Nearly three-quarters of the country's electricity was derived from coal-burning power stations in 1987–88. Thus the future of coal-mining in the region had become closely linked to the needs of the

Table 4.1 *The British coal industry, 1947–89*

	1947	1955	1960	1965/66	1975/76	1979/80	1981/82	1983/84	1985/86	1987/88	1988/89
Output *(million tonnes)*											
Total	200.0	225.2	196.7	185.7	125.8	123.3	124.3	105.3	104.5	99.6	85.0
Of which opencast	10.4	11.6	7.7	6.9	10.4	13.0	14.3	13.8	14.1	15.1	16.8
Consumption *(million tonnes)*											
Inland	187.5	218.7	199.9	184.0	122.2	128.4	117.0	111.7	118.4	115.5	109.2
Imports	0.7	11.8	–	–	4.8	5.1	4.2	5.1	12.1	9.8	12.0
Power stations	27.5	43.6	52.7	69.9	75.8	89.1	85.3	82.3	86.0	86.2	80.7
Collieries											
No. at year end	958	850	698	483	241	219	200	170	133	94	86
Labour											
Colliery employees *(thousands)*	703.9	698.7	602.1	455.7	247.1	232.5	218.5	191.5	154.6	104.4	80.1
Average age *(years)*	n/a	40.4	41.6	43.3	43.2	39.6	39.1	37.9	36.8	34.0	n/a
Output *(per man year, tonnes)*	267	302	310	387	462	470	497	470	571	789	978
Fatal accidents											
	n/a	408	316	217	59	31	34	22	27	9	18
Per 100,000 shifts	n/a	0.24	0.22	0.22	0.11	0.06	0.07	0.05	0.07	0.03	0.07
Dispute losses *(million tonnes)*	1.7	3.3	1.6	1.2	0.5	0.9	1.1	13.1	1.0	4.5	0.6
Earnings *(£ per week)*	6.65	12.46	14.70	19.14	74	119	156	160	194	229	269

n/a = not available

Source: British Coal.

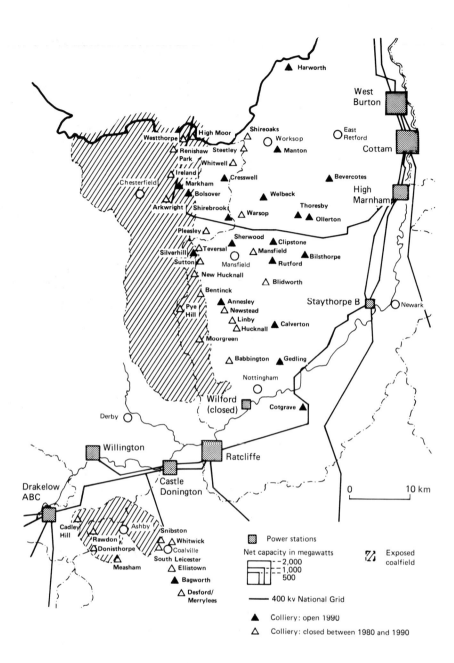

Fig. 4.4. *Coal and power in the East Midlands, 1990.*
Source: Based on Brazier et al (eds), *A New Geography of Nottingham*, Trent Polytechnic 1988, and British Coal data.

electricity industry. As we saw in Chapter 3, the generation of electricity is also heavily concentrated in the East Midlands. This can be seen in detail in Fig. 4.4.

The future of the region's mines became national news in 1984 when the miners' strike was called on the issue of pit closures. The dispute was a bitter one dividing mining communities in the East Midlands. Many Nottinghamshire miners disagreed with the leadership of the National Union of Mineworkers (NUM). One result of the dispute was a new East Midlands based union, the Union of Democratic Mineworkers (UDM). In the late 1980s government policies continued to affect the region's mining communities. The National Coal Board became the British Coal Corporation. This was seen as a pointer to the future privatisation of the industry and this was promised at the Conservative Party conference in 1988. By then the industry was changing rapidly as British Coal's Chairman indicated in the Corporation's 1988 Annual Report.

> Market conditions continue to be the fiercest I have experienced during my business career and, regrettably, collieries clearly unable to produce coal at competitive prices have had to close . . . The main uncertainty which British Coal currently faces remains the impact of the privatisation of the electricity supply industry.
>
> Sir Robert Haslam, 1988

Many nationalised mines in the region and elsewhere were operated at a loss after 1947 because successive governments believed this was in the national interest. (See Chapter 6 for protection policies in agriculture.) However, again political views have changed and uneconomic pits are not attractive to future private owners. Early in 1989 the press reported more contraction of the industry in the region, which it related to privatisation.

> Sudden setbacks in British Coal's drive towards profitability are behind a flurry of 'streamlining' which yesterday saw the number of mining job cuts announced within three weeks rise to nearly 4,000 . . . the backdrop to the drama is the need for coal to show healthy profits in preparation for privatisation. Ironically, the moderate UDM's heartland of Nottinghamshire is the hardest hit . . . Yesterday's announcement that the workforce of Cotgrave Colliery, near Nottingham, would be halved to 550 brought the total job-losses announced in the county's coalfield in just over a week to 1,770.
>
> *Yorkshire Post*, January 1989

However, the shift to deeper mines in the east of the region continued in the 1980s. After much disagreement about the environmental effects of sinking large new mines in rural Leicestershire, work began in the Vale of Belvoir (Fig. 4.5). The intention was to produce 3 million tonnes of coal from the new deep mine at Asfordby by 1993/94. However, by 1990 there were major doubts about the future of the coal industry in the region. The privatisation of the power stations raised difficult questions about importing cheaper, 'cleaner' coal with lower environmental costs. British Coal announced that a further 6,000 jobs would be lost in Nottinghamshire and Yorkshire by 1991. Thus political policies leading to the private ownership of the coal and power industries and tighter controls on pollution from coal burning may well determine the future of the region's 'migrating mines'.

Despite the closure of mines, new opencast sites have appeared on the old concealed field, as modern technology makes it profitable to work remaining shallow deposits. British Coal publicity stresses the economic benefits and the careful planning to minimise inconvenience and damage to the environment. However, new mining operations, particularly opencast activities, are rarely popular with people living near them. Again there are conflicts of interest concerning the best use of the land in the region (see page 42).

Certainly the mining landscape of the East Midlands in the year 2000 will be very different from that of 1900. Since the first industrial revolution, Britain has lost its empire but become a democracy. Attitudes have changed about rocks and riches. In the 1990s, political views are sharply divided about public and private ownership of basic

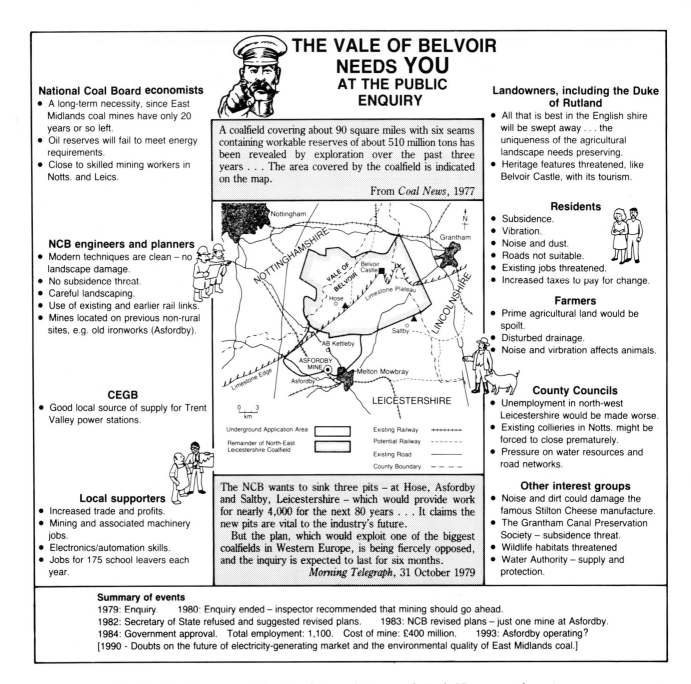

Fig. 4.5. *The Vale of Belvoir dispute.*

industries like coal, iron and steel. However, there is more agreement on the need to repair as much as possible of the damage done to the environment by mining.

Restoring the ruins

In 1990 the Department of the Environment (DOE) classified 46,500 hectares of land in England and Wales as 'derelict'. Most of this was a result of entrepreneurs extracting rocks and minerals over the previous two centuries. Coal waste tips accounted for about 8,000 hectares. It is now public policy to reclaim this land for useful purposes such as agriculture, commercial developments and recreation.

British COAL Opencast Executive

Opencast mining is an efficient method of extracting prime coal reserves in seams too shallow or too thin to be worked safely and economically by underground mining.

Opencast mining plays a vital role in the low-cost recovery of shallow reserves. The coal costs less per tonne to produce than deep-mined coal. Several seams can be worked at the same time.

Topsoil and subsoil are removed separately. Some of the soil can be placed in mounds called 'baffle banks' which act as a barrier for noise and dust, as well as providing a visual screen for the site.

Rocks overlying the coal seams (the overburden) are excavated efficiently by draglines, but hard rock may have to be blasted.

The coal is extracted very carefully to ensure that no rock is mixed with it before it goes to be crushed, sized and blended at the coal disposal point.

When the removal of coal is finished, the overburden is replaced to agreed contours and the subsoil and topsoil are re-spread.

It is possible to restore land to a variety of after-uses. Most land goes to agriculture but it may be restored to forestry, recreational areas (country parks and nature reserves), industrial or residential development.

Opencast mining and land reclamation.

It's war on BC's opencast digging
Village's rally call to region

TOWNS and villages throughout the East Midlands were last night urged to stand united in a concerted effort to end British Coal's view of the region as "a large opencast pit."

Individual communities faced with outcropping were simply "bleating in the wind" when they battled alone against BC's well-funded professional approach, Mr Maurice Cresswell told Cossall's annual parish meeting.

About 350 acres of green belt countryside, from Cossalls award-winning conservation area to the M1 at Trowell, is soon to be prospected to test the economic viability of digging out an estimated three million tonnes of coal.

If the go-ahead for the Robinettes site is given, it will be the fifth opencast operation in the parish over the last four years and the latest in a whole series along the Erewash Valley.

The scheme to re-use a former colliery site near Coalville in the older part of the Leicestershire field is a good example of modern attitudes to restoring the ruins. The press extract shown here reflects the local issues involved.

Changing face of COALVILLE

With the help of British Coal's Enterprise scheme, work is well under way on the conversion of the Snibston colliery pit baths into a new, sleek complex of office suites.

Cows are now grazing on the familiar slag heaps of Snibston Colliery.

The cattle are part of a mammoth programme to reclaim the land near the town centre, once used as the pit's tipping site.

Leicestershire County Council have announced a £3.7 million plan to transform the Snibston Colliery site in Coalville into an industrial heritage museum and leisure complex.

There has been a rash of applications for a 55,000 sq.ft. area of non-food shopping space to be built in conjunction with the proposed museum and recreation area on the old Snibston Colliery site.

Snibston Colliery Reclamation Scheme, Coalville.
Source: Leicester Mercury, 8 July 1987.

1 Referring to Table 4.1, write a short account of the major changes that have occurred in the British coalmining industry since 1947, indicating how you think these have affected life and the landscape in the East Midlands.

2 Predicting the future is more difficult. Using the material in this chapter, write a short article for a local newspaper under the headline, 'Coal in the East Midlands, AD 2000'.

Summary

- The geological variety of the East Midlands is the source of many mineral resources. Where, when and how these have been exploited has depended on the growth of human knowledge, technological development and market forces.

- The exploitation of coal and iron in the west of the region helped to create the first industrial revolution in Britain. This process had a major effect on lifestyles and the landscape in the East Midlands.

- The exhaustion of the shallower coal seams has led to a shift of mining to the east. Important social and political changes are associated with these movements.

- Changes in social attitudes and political views have led to new policies about repairing industrial damage to the British environment. Restoring and re-using land in the region's mining areas are now important factors in the further evolution of the East Midlands landscape.

5 Water, wheels and wings

We know that nearly 2,000 years ago the Romans built a system of straight, paved roads across the region. These were designed to move soldiers quickly between fortified towns like Lincoln (Lindum) and Leicester (Ratae). However, moving goods was another matter. It was easier and much cheaper by boat. The Romans knew all about this. They used rivers and a canal to make Lincoln an important trading centre. In the early Middle Ages, Boston, at the mouth of the Witham, was the country's second port. It still has one of the largest parish churches in England. This was built largely with money from wool exported to Europe through the port.

Thus the different ways used to move people and their goods – over land, by water and by air – at different times have had a great influence on the region. They have left their mark on the landscape, and changed the ways of life here.

Prime positions

Boston is no longer one of Britain's major ports. However, following the boundary changes of 1974, it has the only sizeable dock in the five counties. The modern port dates from the river improvements and dock construction of the 1880s. It was based on the then new railway system of the East Midlands rather than on river transport. In 1988 over 90 per cent of the port's traffic was moved by road. However, it is Boston's geographical position that remains the basis for a flourishing minor port (Fig. 5.1 and Table 5.1). The 1985 *Port Handbook*

Table 5.1 *Port of Boston traffic trends, 1980–85 (thousand tonnes)*

	1980	1985
Inwards,	666.7	755.0
of which		
Steel	357.9	273.6
Paper	84.4	153.8
Timber	63.1	144.1
Animal feed	45.2	20.7
General cargo	38.2	137.0
Coal and coke	7.4	20.0
Outwards,	309.0	707.6
of which		
Grain	193.2	632.9
General cargo	58.8	67.6
Total	975.7	1,462.6

Source: Port of Boston Authority.

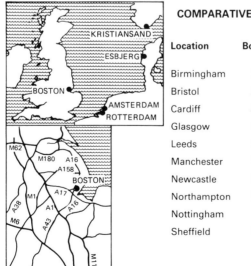

COMPARATIVE ROAD DISTANCE TABLES (km)

Location	Boston	Immingham	Felixstowe	Hull
Birmingham	167	214	269	219
Bristol	299	364	338	365
Cardiff	346	396	396	396
Glasgow	494	441	668	394
Leeds	167	114	339	95
Manchester	180	175	352	154
Newcastle	301	243	470	195
Northampton	117	241	187	253
Nottingham	87	122	240	146
Sheffield	125	101	301	108

Fig. 5.1. *Port of Boston, 1985.*
Source: Port of Boston Authority.

stresses Boston's central location, a theme that runs through this chapter.

> Boston now claims to be one of the most successful small ports in Britain . . . [it] continues to break all its cargo handling records, and throughput has now tripled in only 15 years . . .
>
> Boston is arguably the most centrally located port on the whole of the English east coast. In terms of nearness to its direct **hinterland** in the Midlands, no other English port on the east coast is closer. However, it has additional advantages in that it is competitively located for both the industrial north of England and the prime areas of London, Bristol and South Wales . . .
>
> The port's cargo profile is well hedged, with four **liner services** . . . together with a well diversified bulk profile which includes grain, steel, timber and forestry products.

---

hinterland
The area from which a port derives its trade.

liner services
Regular shipping services operating to a timetable between specified ports carrying container traffic. That is, cargo is carried in large metal boxes of a standard size designed for rail or road haulage.

Between 1890 and 1980, Boston changed completely from a railway port to one dominated by road haulage. In 1988 the management plan was to reduce the road-hauled trade to 75 per cent. Write a report for the Port Authority describing trade trends in the 1980s and justifying the proposed change in transport policy.

Nodes and networks

The regular movements of people and goods result in communication systems linking population centres or sources of materials, for example a mine. These links and centres form patterns on or over the land. In geography we call these patterns **networks**. To understand the modern transport networks of the East Midlands we need to know about previous patterns.

---

network
In geography consists of links between centres. These links are called *edges* or *arcs*; the centres are termed *nodes*. A node is also known as a *vertex* (plural *vertices*). The efficiency with which vertices are connected is known as the *connectivity of the network*.

Navigations and navvies

We know that it was easy for early invaders to enter and cross the East Midlands by water. The Romans cut the region's first known canal to link Lincoln on the River Witham with the Trent and thus the Humber Estuary. The Fossdyke has survived and is still in use today. The Trent, the region's largest river, has been used from prehistoric times. Dugout canoes dating from 1000 BC have been found near Nottingham. There is evidence of commercial use of the river by Romans, Danes and Normans. However, the Trent also illustrates the problems of transport networks based on natural waterways. Few British rivers are without obstructions like rapids and sandbanks. By the 18th century they had to be improved. Poor transport was holding back the economy.

Acts of Parliament were passed to allow companies to improve rivers and create efficient 'navigations'. The Trent Navigation Act was passed in 1699 with another in 1794 to allow locks and weirs along a hundred miles of 'navigation' (Fig 5.2). Unfortunately this system, the region's major waterway, was not completed until 1926. By then other networks had taken over.

However, nationally the cuts or canals were the real transport breakthrough of the industrial revolution. By 1800 great construction gangs of 'navvies' were criss-crossing England creating a new transport network. The East Midlands was soon part of the first transport network which could support Britain as an industrial nation.

> Most of the amazing work of the 'navvies' remains, though some canals have been filled in. Find out all you can about any canals in your area. Choose any of these and write an article for a local newspaper describing its building and opening. Your local library may be able to help you with microfilm of the newspapers of the day.

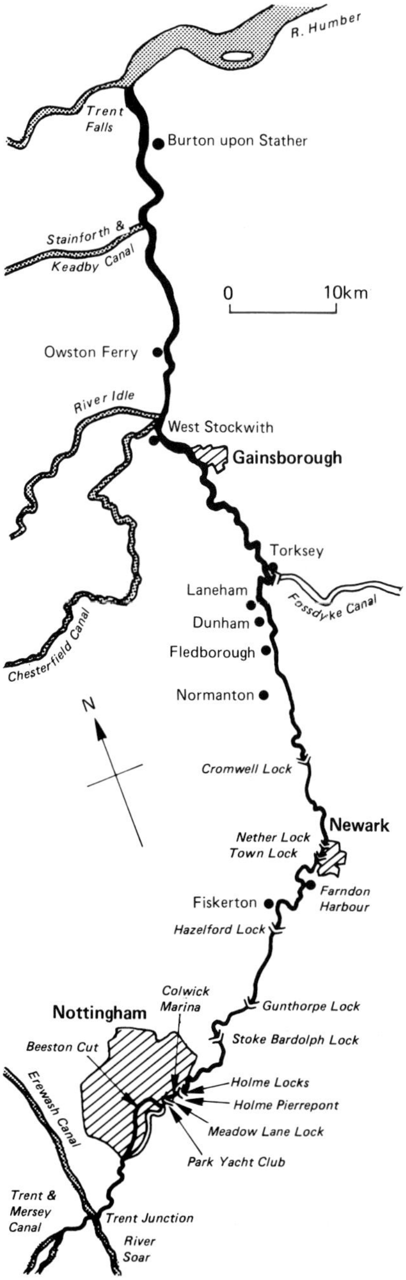

Turnpikes, tolls and tickets

Transport networks change as a result of economic demand and improved technology. Britain experienced an economic boom in the 18th century. We have seen that transport had to be improved. One result was the navigations; another was the system of turnpike roads. Groups of landowners and business people got together to improve old roads, often dating from the Romans, and to build new ones. They used a system of tolls or charges paid by road users to finance this new network.

The toll roads, or turnpikes, created a new transport network. This brought the coaching age which lasted for about a century. The national system of fast coaches hauled by teams of horses brought a new transport industry and prosperity to many towns in the East Midlands. The great coaches with names like the 'North Briton' crossed the region linking Scotland and the North with London. Coaching inns served the same functions as today's modern motorway service stations. Many workers and trades were needed to keep the coaches running. Coaching changed the ways of life in towns like Stamford, Grantham, Newark, Blyth and Bawtry on or near the Great North Road.

> Find out all you can about coaching in your area. Look for evidence of coaching inns. Many retain the large entrances that were big enough for a coach. Make a list of the jobs associated with the coach network. Write an illustrated account of a day in the life of a passenger or driver.

Coaching lasted for about a century until the 1840s when the railway companies made it obsolete with their new network. The iron horse on rails was faster and cheaper than real horses pulling coaches on toll roads. The transport market changed again. The coaching towns of the region declined or became railway centres. Railway tickets replaced turnpike tolls. Canals and navigations did not decline as swiftly. The Trent Navigation still functions but in a limited way.

The railway age was not only vital to the industrial revolution. It also brought a transport revolution which altered ways of life and work. By 1900 most people in the East Midlands were able to travel beyond the range of the horse and cart. There was greater choice than ever before about where to live, work and play. However, economic change and new technology were to bring new systems by the middle of this century. People were to become even more mobile, but the rail system had to contract as petrol-driven wheels and wings changed the transport geography of the East Midlands.

Fig. 5.2. *Trent Navigation, 1985.*
Source: *Motor Boat and Yachting*, August 1985.

Steam, service stations and sprinters

The rail network spread across the region and many different companies were involved. But by the middle of the 20th century, competition from the new public road network led to its contraction. Economic difficulties and political changes led to the nationalisation of the railways in 1947. British Railways (BR) replaced the old private companies. Since the Second World War the British railway system has been cut by about one half (Fig. 5.3). In 1937 there were 33,940 km of track. In 1988 there were 17,339 km. The main closures were in the 1960s. Since then BR has invested heavily in its smaller network. It replaced steam trains by diesel units in the 1960s and began to electrify main lines in the 1970s and '80s. The mid-1980s saw the modernisation of local services with new diesel 'Sprinter' trains.

At the same time, the trunk road and motorway system was developed. Since the 1960s there have been fast road links in north–south directions across the west and centre of the East Midlands region (Fig. 5.4). However, east–west driving is much slower, especially in parts of Derbyshire, Leicestershire and Lincolnshire. The progress of the M42 into the region from the West Midlands was also slow, and the link with the M1 at Kegworth was not completed until the early 1990s.

To a large extent the M1 and A1 throughways duplicate the main inter-city rail links through the East Midlands. The old railway companies competed with each other for profitable routes to London. This competition and physical problems left some major centres in the region with weak direct-rail links. That is, they were not on the main north–south lines (Fig. 5.5). The time-distance map (Fig. 5.6) shows this clearly.

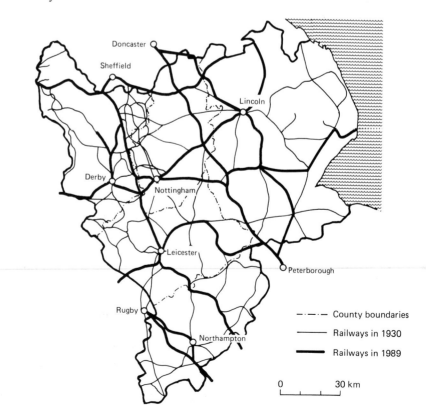

Fig. 5.3. *Growth and contraction of the East Midlands rail network.*
Source: Based on British Rail data.

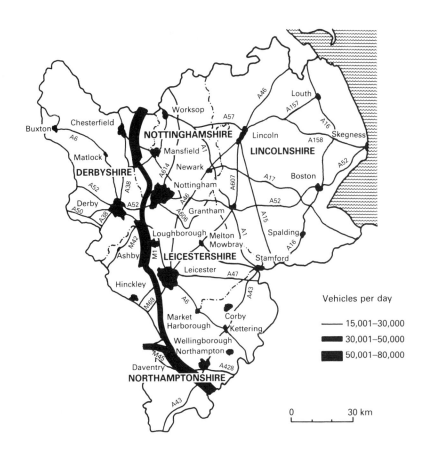

Fig. 5.4. *East Midlands road system and motorway flows, 1986.*
Source: Based on Ministry of Transport data.

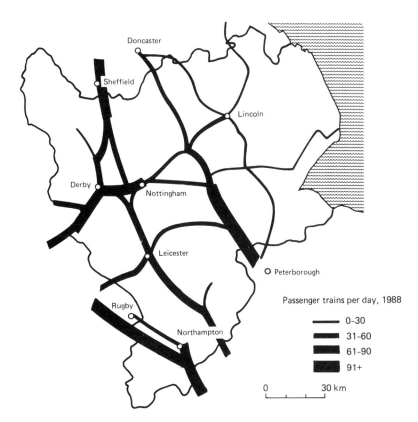

Fig. 5.5. *Rail flows in the East Midlands, 1988.*
Source: Based on British Rail data.

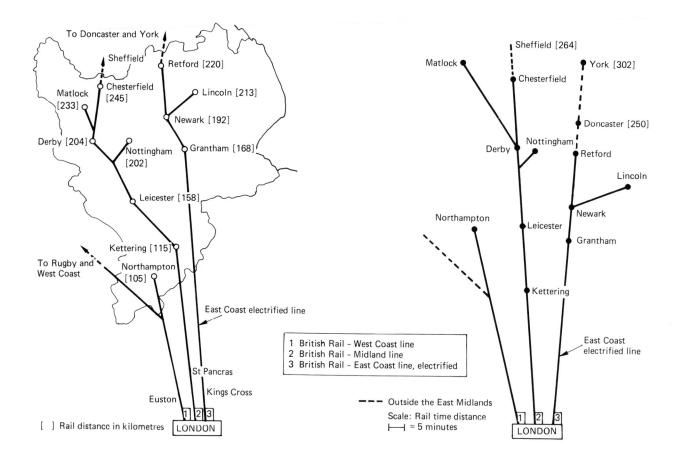

Fig. 5.6. *Rail access to London from the East Midlands, 1988.*
Source: Based on British Rail data.

1 Which major centres in the region are not on main lines from London connecting directly with the north?
2 Imagine you have been appointed sales manager of a company selling throughout the East Midlands. You will visit your customers by car but must go to your London head office at least once a week. Your company will help you to buy a house provided it is well located for your job. Write a memo to your director explaining where you intend to live, and why.

The old, privately financed railway system did not leave the region with a network serving all its major centres efficiently. By the late 1980s BR was trying to improve the effectiveness of its East Midlands network, especially in relation to the largest city, Nottingham. In May 1988 it introduced new, direct Sprinter services between the nodes that had never been linked effectively by rail before (Fig. 5.7).

Write short articles for local newspapers in each of the five counties reporting on BR's new provincial cross-country services in May 1988. Give the editor's views on the quality of rail transport in his or her county.

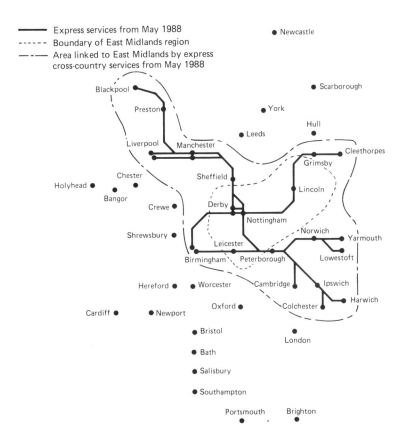

Fig. 5.7. *Provincial rail network and the East Midlands, 1988.*
Source: Based on British Rail data.

From bomber bases to BMA

British Midlands Airways (BMA) had become Britain's third largest airline by 1985. It is based at the East Midlands International Airport (EMIA) at Castle Donington, a former RAF airfield in north-east Leicestershire.

'We certainly feel at the centre of things on this shift,' said Mick Henshall, the Ramp Duty Officer at the EMIA. It was just before midnight as we talked to him in his control room high above the 'apron' or aircraft parking area.

The EMIA at night.

51

The EMIA is one of Britain's two 'hub and spoke' centres for the rapid transit of letters and parcels. The Post Office uses Speke Airport, Liverpool, and the EMIA as the air transport 'hubs' for its air, road and rail distribution system.

The EMIA was opened in 1965 and came of age on 1 April 1986, 21 years after the first airport authority was formed by five local authorities. Nottingham and Derby Corporations had realised that their small civic airports were inadequate for the coming age of air transport. They joined with Derbyshire, Leicestershire and Nottinghamshire County Councils to set up a regional airport. Castle Donington was chosen as the best available site (Fig. 5.8).

The EMIA is Britain's newest major airport. From 1979 to 1984 it had the country's fastest growth in air movements. The miners' strike caused a temporary drop in holiday passengers but growth resumed in 1986.

Mick Henshall has seen most of the changes at the EMIA since the late '60s (Fig. 5.9). He is now one of 6 duty officers whose 13-man crews handle all aircraft on the ground around the clock.

Fig. 5.8. *East Midlands International Airport – location and accessibility.*
Source: Based on EMIA data.

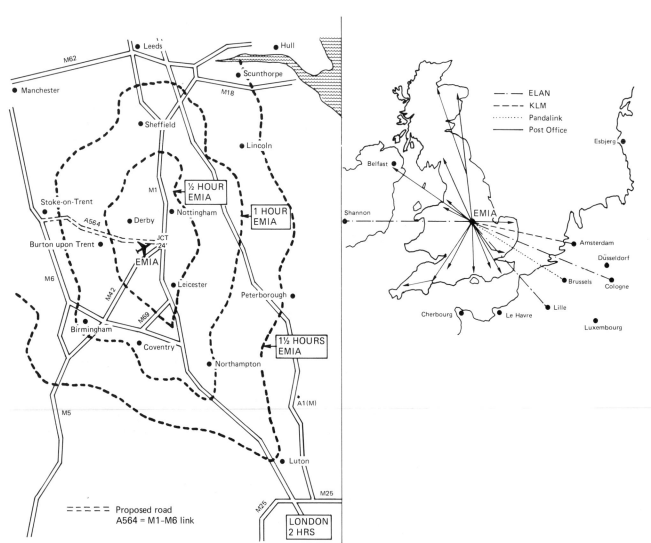

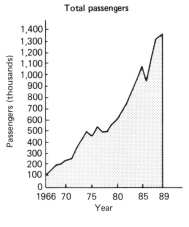

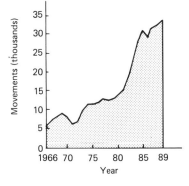

Fig. 5.9. *Growth of the EMIA.*
Source: Based on EMIA data.

I can give you some data on a typical 24-hour period. Here's a computer print-out showing 172 aircraft arrivals and departures. You can see that the busiest shift is 18.00 to midnight with 74 movements. In fact, we had 60 between 21.30 and 02.30. Tonight will be even busier because it's Friday. On top of 50-plus mail and freight flights, we've got seven charters to Greece or Spain. They're all Boeing 737s, which means over a thousand holiday-makers going through here in about three hours.

We have to be on our toes to keep the apron working smoothly, especially if we get some more diversions. During the 1988 postal strike with Speke hardly working, we had 74 diversions in three weeks. Then there are Jumbo 747s diverted to us by bad weather over London. Our conditions are usually better and with the M1 so close we can move passengers on quickly by coach. It's all good extra business, like the flight simulators which bring aircrew here for training.

It's not surprising we now have the Donington Thistle Hotel next to our modernised Terminal Building. In fact, we are now the most central major airport in the country and in the top four for freight. This has brought a lot of jobs. There are about 3,500 people working here, with another thousand or so linked to us in the area. Many are highly skilled and well paid, so we are something of an economic growth spot in the East Midlands. It gives people a lot of new chances. I'm a case in point. I used to be in farming!

---

1 On 1 April 1987 the EMIA was privatised and became a public limited company in line with Conservative Government policy. The only shareholders in the present company are Derbyshire, Leicestershire and Nottinghamshire County Councils, and Nottingham City Council. This situation could change with further government legislation, or if a shareholder decides to sell shares. Politically, there are different views on the advantages and disadvantages of public and private ownership of airports like the EMIA. Draft short speeches which might be given by local councillors supporting or opposing the privatisation of the EMIA.
2 The EMIA is located in north-east Leicestershire. The County Council's policy is to try to improve job prospects in the area by encouraging new industries and service enterprises on or near the airport. Design a brochure which Leicestershire County Council could use to attract such activities.

Summary

- We can think of the movement of people and materials across and within the East Midlands in terms of networks. These have changed as technology and the economy have developed. To understand modern networks we must study previous patterns.

- We can explain these former networks and how they developed by considering the technology, market forces and political factors that have operated at various times in the region.

- The region's economy and lifestyles now depend more on road transport than on rail networks. However, there are major differences in the transport services available in different parts of the East Midlands, so investment in transport is an important political issue.

- The region also has an important place in Britain's civil air network.

6 Ploughs, profits and politics

The 'English shires' suggests a green, fertile area. To some extent this image is correct. The East Midlands region occupies less than one-tenth of the UK but usually produces one-fifth of its wheat and sugar beet. It has about an eighth of the national potato crop and a tenth of the barley grown. About 80 per cent of the region's land is used for agriculture, but this is farmed by less than 3 per cent of its workforce.

As Fig. 6.1 indicates, between Buxton and Boston there is a cross-section of English farming. This variety is based on the different physical landscapes identified in Chapter 3, but farming landscapes are not permanent. How and why they change is important not only for economic reasons but because they form so much of our national environment (Table 6.1).

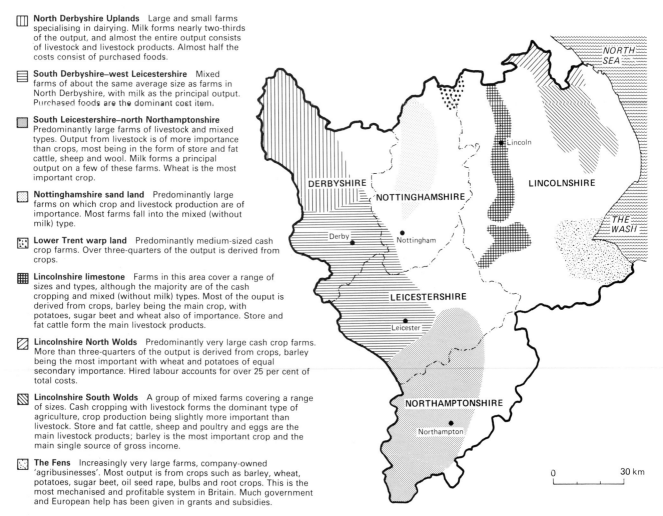

Fig. 6.1. *Distinct agricultural areas in the East Midlands.*
Source: Based on data supplied by R. O. Wood.

- **North Derbyshire Uplands** Large and small farms specialising in dairying. Milk forms nearly two-thirds of the output, and almost the entire output consists of livestock and livestock products. Almost half the costs consist of purchased foods.

- **South Derbyshire–west Leicestershire** Mixed farms of about the same average size as farms in North Derbyshire, with milk as the principal output. Purchased foods are the dominant cost item.

- **South Leicestershire–north Northamptonshire** Predominantly large farms of livestock and mixed types. Output from livestock is of more importance than crops, most being in the form of store and fat cattle, sheep and wool. Milk forms a principal output on a few of these farms. Wheat is the most important crop.

- **Nottinghamshire sand land** Predominantly large farms on which crop and livestock production are of importance. Most farms fall into the mixed (without milk) type.

- **Lower Trent warp land** Predominantly medium-sized cash crop farms. Over three-quarters of the output is derived from crops.

- **Lincolnshire limestone** Farms in this area cover a range of sizes and types, although the majority are of the cash cropping and mixed (without milk) types. Most of the ouput is derived from crops, barley being the main crop, with potatoes, sugar beet and wheat also of importance. Store and fat cattle form the main livestock products.

- **Lincolnshire North Wolds** Predominantly very large cash crop farms. More than three-quarters of the output is derived from crops, barley being the most important with wheat and potatoes of equal secondary importance. Hired labour accounts for over 25 per cent of total costs.

- **Lincolnshire South Wolds** A group of mixed farms covering a range of sizes. Cash cropping with livestock forms the dominant type of agriculture, crop production being slightly more important than livestock. Store and fat cattle, sheep and poultry and eggs are the main livestock products; barley is the most important crop and the main single source of gross income.

- **The Fens** Increasingly very large farms, company-owned 'agribusinesses'. Most output is from crops such as barley, wheat, potatoes, sugar beet, oil seed rape, bulbs and root crops. This is the most mechanised and profitable system in Britain. Much government and European help has been given in grants and subsidies.

Table 6.1 *East Midlands agriculture, 1985*

	% land used for agriculture	% occupations in agriculture	% farmland arable	% farmland permanent pasture	% farms rough grazing
Derbyshire	70.1	1.7	32.1	50.4	17.5
Leicestershire	77.8	1.7	64.7	34.1	1.2
Lincolnshire	87.4	10.2	89.5	9.6	0.9
Northamptonshire	80.9	2.3	71.5	27.8	0.7
Nottinghamshire	71.2	1.5	83.8	15.4	0.8

Source: Ministry of Agriculture.

Table 6.2 *Changes in agricultural land use in the East Midlands, 1971–82*

		Agric. area as % of total	% of farmland Ploughed each year	Under cereals	Under permanent pasture
Derbyshire*	1971	74.7	18.9	15.1	53.3
	1982	70.1	20.4	17.4	51.2
Leicestershire	1971	77.9	44.5	39.1	40.7
	1982	77.8	50.5	44.0	35.8
Lincolnshire*	1971	86.9	79.2	53.3	13.5
	1982	87.4	83.2	57.5	10.0
Northamptonshire	1971	82.8	51.8	45.6	34.8
	1982	80.9	59.7	50.9	29.7
Nottinghamshire	1971	72.1	63.7	51.1	22.3
	1982	71.1	71.5	53.7	18.2
England	1971	73.7	42.9	31.9	32.1
	1982	72.6	49.7	35.8	33.0

* county boundaries changed in 1974

Source: Ministry of Agriculture.

European (Economic) Community Common Agricultural Policy
The EEC or Common Market was formed in 1958 by Belgium, France, Italy, Luxembourg, the Netherlands and West Germany (the Six). Denmark, the Republic of Ireland and the UK joined in 1973, Greece in 1980 and Spain and Portugal in 1986. The group is now more often referred to as the European Community (EC). The basic aim of the Community was to strengthen trade links between member states, but CAP is part of an attempt to co-ordinate social, financial and economic policies. Because farming systems vary so much within the EC, it is difficult to get agreement on CAP, but in 1990 a decision was made to reduce financial support to EC agriculture by 30 per cent.

free market
Most businesses operate in situations where government does not directly fix costs and prices. This is known as a free market. However, taxes and regulations leave few business transactions totally free of interference. Many economists regard the free market as more of an idea than a reality.

Since 1973 British farmers have worked under the rules of the **Common Agricultural Policy** (CAP) of the **European Community** (EC) or 'Common Market'. These have helped to change agriculture in the region (Table 6.2). Many farmers have found it more profitable to use their land in new ways within the Market. This has changed much of our rural environment. People have different views on these changes. Agricultural land use is now an important political issue.

In this chapter we will investigate the region's changing patterns of agriculture by considering farming as a system adjusting to new conditions. We will examine farms as businesses which must make a profit but do not operate in a **free market**.

Make a list of the ways in which East Midlands farmers changed their land use in the decade after Britain joined the EC. Write brief comments on the changes from the points of view of a farmer, a housewife and a naturalist.

system
In geography, consists of parts or components connected so that something is done or produced. It has inputs and outputs linked by a flow of energy through the process of the system. Most systems studied in geography are *open* because they receive energy and materials from the environment and *feed back* into it. Thus they are always adjusting to the changing conditions around them.

Farming as a system

It is useful to think of farming in the region as a **system** designed to produce food and materials for profit (Fig. 6.2). Farming is an open system with human and physical inputs. An individual farm is a business. It is the basic unit of production in the system. Its fields, buildings, machines and other resources are linked by the farmer's management to make a profit. Some outputs are fed back into the system and may help to modify it. If it is to work well as a business system, farming must adjust continually to its economic environment, and especially to market demands.

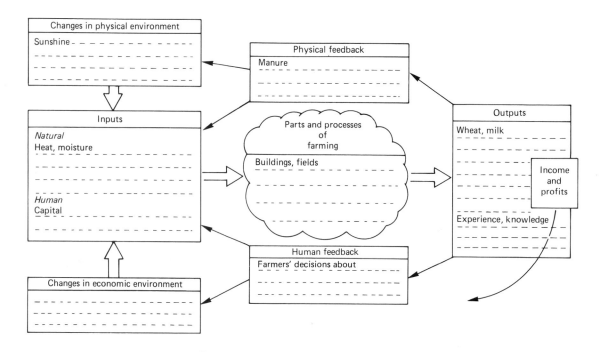

Fig. 6.2. *Farming as a system.*

Complete Fig. 6.2 by putting words or symbols in the spaces.

productivity
The efficiency with which inputs are used to produce goods in an economic system. It is often measured by dividing the output by the number of workers. For example, the productivity of a dairy farm might be calculated by relating milk production to the labour costs.

Changing the system

Farming systems have changed greatly in Britain and the East Midlands in this century (Fig. 6.3 and Table 6.3). Two World Wars brought major changes. By 1914 Britain imported much of her food. In both wars these food imports were threatened by submarine campaigns. Governments were forced to interfere in the farming system to increase production.

No government since the war has been willing to allow back a free market. All have used public money to ensure a strong farming system. They have subsidised input costs and guaranteed output prices. The CAP has done this on a bigger scale (see Table 6.5). At the same time more and better machines have replaced human labour. Advanced technology, e.g. improved breeds, seeds and pest control, has greatly increased **productivity**.

Fig. 6.3. *Changing farm inputs in Britain, 1938–75.*
Source: Based on Ministry of Agriculture data.

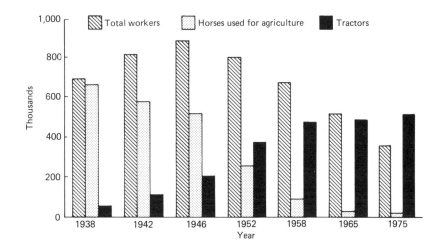

Table 6.3 *Changes in East Midlands agriculture, 1939–65*

		Farms (thousands)	Employees (thousands)	Wheat yield (cwt per acre)	Cattle (thousands)	Sheep (thousands)
Derbyshire	1939	8.33	8.14	17.5	168.2	147.8
	1965	7.12	5.07	30.7	311.7	756.8
Leicestershire	1939	5.36	14.80	17.5	164.6	266.6
	1965	4.75	4.72	32.6	180.6	283.5
Lincolnshire	1939	18.62	41.17	20.8	244.4	570.0
	1965	14.47	26.43	35.6	242.0	483.8
Northamptonshire	1939	4.45	8.21	16.2	152.0	384.5
	1965	3.34	4.59	32.4	143.3	350.0
Nottinghamshire	1939	5.40	8.01	16.7	99.4	142.9
	1965	4.34	5.17	31.4	114.2	121.4
England	1939	303.64	564.49	19.1*	5,911.5*	13,337.2*
	1965	269.97	348.01	32.4*	8,791.1*	20,250.1*

* England and Wales

Source: Ministry of Agriculture.

Band Aid
Charity set up by pop stars, particularly Bob Geldof, to raise money for the relief of famine in Third World countries in the mid-1980s.

food mountain
Popular name for stores of agricultural products bought up under the CAP of the EC to prevent a fall in prices. The UK had 5 million tonnes of grain stored in 1986. Following drought and bad harvests in North America, it was reported that this national grain mountain had been reduced to 'a 500,000-tonne foothill' by the end of 1988.

Higher agricultural productivity and bigger farms have changed much of the countryside. Not everyone is happy about these changes. Many British taxpayers find it hard to understand why we need **Band Aid** when we have **food mountains**. Many British farmers know that they have benefited from the protected farming system but they did not create it and they do not control it. Most farms are individual business units. The individual farmer in the East Midlands knows that political policies can change his business and lifestyle very quickly. Each farm business is different, but they tend to form groups within the region. Table 6.4 reflects this. It is based on real farms across the East Midlands.

> Look again at Fig. 6.1 and Table 6.4, and try to explain why some areas seem to support more profitable farms than others.

Table 6.4 Farms and finance in the East Midlands, 1986 – average inputs/outputs for farming systems and areas

	Dairying (Derbys.)	Arable/dairying (Derbys. & Leics.)	Arable/cereals (Notts. & Lincs.)	Arable/cereals & roots (Lincs.)	Beef/sheep (Northants.)
No. of farms sampled	11	9	14	19	18
Av. size (hectares)	33.75	355.75	337.25	313.25	58.75
Av. no. of cattle	113	335	179	103	187
Av. no. of ewes	–	231	195	97	100
Av. arable area (ha)	–	211	245	265	19
Av. grass area (ha)	34	132	82	37	39
Inputs/costs	£	£	£	£	£
Purchased feed	24,232	48,005	10,421	8,831	5,904
Livestock costs	3,139	9,406	4,711	2,572	1,847
Fertilizers	3,674	35,543	30,551	32,190	2,270
Sprays	169	15,923	15,210	19,525	330
Other crop costs	439	15,464	12,886	24,104	828
Contract work	945	3,920	5,197	5,028	790
Labour	5,062	64,462	34,416	45,396	4,080
Equipment & power	8,572	58,532	50,520	56,864	5,003
Overheads & rent	7,662	59,934	47,891	47,566	8,123
Total inputs	53,894	311,189	211,803	242,076	29,175
Outputs/sales					
Livestock	9,216	56,974	56,553	31,350	25,722
Milk	52,682	101,904	–	–	–
Cereals, incl. rape	–	188,277	214,356	162,753	5,003
Roots (beet, potatoes)	–	–	*	92,380	–
Other income	877	9,356	7,703	9,792	1,487
Total outputs	62,775	356,511	278,612	296,275	32,212
Surplus/profit	8,876	45,322	66,809	54,199	3,037

Note: Area under crops and grass is not the total area – there are also woods, roads, etc. * negligible

Source: R. O. Wood.

Staying in business

Talking to a real farmer in Derbyshire about the way he runs his business helps us to understand the changing patterns in the region. John Winder has been farming near Matlock for about 30 years:

> We married on 25th March 1963 and moved to High Leas the same week. We rented 80 acres – enough for 20 milk cows. I'd worked on local farms since leaving school and done two years at agricultural college. I came back here to set up on my own after managing a dairy farm in Cheshire. We hadn't much capital and the regular cheques from the Milk Marketing Board kept us afloat for the two years it took to build up the herd. By then I knew my land and realised that by working on improving it, building a covered yard and putting in a silage pit, we could probably double the stock. So I went for all the grants I could get and worked all hours. By 1970 we had 40 Friesians and Ayrshires.
>
> Then came the big decision. My landlord bought Low Leas Farm; we took on another 50 acres! It meant more borrowing, but the chance to milk 80 beasts and to have a cowman. The Ministry thought the land would do it but I soon realised that up here on a long, narrow holding 65 to 70 was the limit. By now we were in Europe, and the Common Market brought higher milk prices. So we did what the Continental farmers had done. We went all out for maximum production. We invested a lot in better stock, machinery and feedstuffs. Yes, the Common Market helped us to raise output but the '70s also brought high inflation, bigger wages, crippling costs and frightening interest rates. True, milk cost you 4p more on the doorstep, but only 1p came my way.
>
> The '80s have brought lower inflation but interest rates have stayed up and could well rise again. There is a lot of opposition to the CAP as it is – the writing's on the wall with milk quotas and other regulations. My output is down by nearly 20 per cent since 1985. Now, paying a hired man, I'm working virtually without wages. Yet, as a widower, I can't manage physically on my own any more. So for now, it's back to 'dog and stick' farming – about 20 beasts and any sidelines I can manage. You can see that after 25 years my business wheel will have turned full circle!

---

1 Read John Winder's story carefully and discuss with your teacher what he means by the following: silage pit; Milk Marketing Board; Friesians and Ayrshires; frightening interest rates; milk quota; 'dog and stick' farming.
2 Ask any farmer you know about his or her experience of the CAP.

---

prairie farming
Popular term for larger-scale farming in Britain in the 1980s. The North American prairies produce great quantities of grain on large, highly mechanised farms. Fields are very large on the prairies and there are few hedges and trees.

conservationist
Person who believes in taking action to protect the environment, particularly to prevent what is considered the unnecessary human destruction of ecological systems. Conservationists are often called 'greens', and some formed the Green Party. Conservation is currently attracting much political and public interest.

Problems of protection

Political policies meant that in 1987 about 70 per cent of British farm output had guaranteed markets and prices for most of its products including cereals, sugar beet, milk and beef. Higher CAP prices, improved seeds and machines together with new crops like oilseed rape brought bigger profits (Fig. 6.4 and Table 6.5).

Thus in a few years political decisions can help to change the farming system and our rural environment. In the East Midlands many farmers have responded to political policies by putting more land under modern methods of cultivation. The changes in other regions, such as East Anglia, have been much greater. There is talk of **prairie farming**, and **conservationists** warn of major damage to the environment as a result of changes in the farming system.

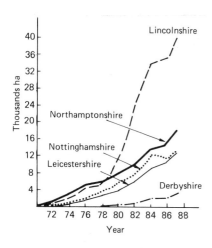

Fig. 6.4. *The increase of oilseed rape in the East Midlands, 1972–87.*
Source: Based on Ministry of Agriculture data.

Table 6.5 *Public money inputs to agriculture from CAP and the British government, 1970–86 (£ millions)*

	1970–71	1980–81	1984–85	1985–86
Market regulations under CAP	Nil	648.3	1,376.7	1,893.0
Price guarantees	174.3	45.5	−0.2	7.8
Improvements support	50.7	205.1	202.9	144.9
Support for special areas	31.5	113.5	129.7	143.1
Other support	Nil	Nil	5.2	26.5
Total	256.5	1,012.4	1,714.3	2,215.3

Source: Central Statistical Office.

So changes in agricultural land use and the farming system are major issues in the 1990s. Political policies designed to protect our food supplies in wartime and to bring European nations together in peace have led to environmental problems and many changes. Government policies and farming practices will adjust to these changes. The face of the countryside will go on changing.

Summary

- More land is used for farming in the East Midlands than for any other purpose, but relatively few people work in agriculture. Across the region agricultural land use varies greatly with physical and other conditions.

- We can think of farming as an open system set up to produce food and material for profit. The agricultural systems in Britain and the East Midlands have changed greatly in this century. Since 1945 farms have tended to become larger and much more productive.

- Individual farms are the basic units of agricultural production. Farmers are business people who use their land to make the best living they can. Their methods vary according to their perceptions of physical conditions, the markets and their knowledge, skills and attitudes.

- The region's farming is also influenced by political decisions. Government interference in the free market resulted from threats to food supplies in two World Wars. Since 1973 the CAP of the EC has been a major political factor in changing agricultural land use and methods. Conservation of the rural environment and control of pollution became major, related issues in the 1980s.

7 Changing patterns and places of work

Advert in the Derby Mercury, 1771.

Richard Arkwright was born in Preston, Lancashire in 1732, the thirteenth child of a tailor. He was apprenticed to a barber and practised the trade in Bolton. In 1769 he invented a machine for spinning cotton, which, since it was powered by water, became known as the Waterframe.

Arkwright's first mill at Cromford was built in 1771 and the whole mill site was finished by 1791. At the same time, he developed Cromford into one of the first industrial villages, including workers' cottages, a market place and a lock-up.

Arkwright's mill, with its powered machinery and large workforce, became the model for others throughout Britain and abroad, earning Arkwright the title "Father of the Factory System".

Richard Arkwright and Cromford.
Source: Arkwright Society.

Fig. 7.1. *Cotton spinning – cottage and factory systems.*

In Chapter 6 we found it useful to think of farming as an economic system. We were trying to understand the changing patterns of agriculture in the East Midlands. Manufacturing is another major economic system, also designed to produce the maximum profit. The system changed the life and landscape in Britain and in many other countries.

Cromford is on the River Derwent, 27 km north of Derby. Before 1771 it was a remote leadmining village. Now thousands of people visit Cromford each year to see one of the places where the Industrial Revolution began. We know that from about 1750 manufacturing based on water and then steam power began to change much of Britain. Richard Arkwright (1732–92) was one of the key figures in these changes. He was born and raised in Lancashire but is remembered for his work in Derbyshire. Richard was the youngest son of a large, poor family and he began work as a barber. He had little education and no qualifications. Yet he became a great industrial inventor and one of the creators of the factory system.

Until Arkwright's time, wool and cotton were spun in people's houses on small spinning-wheels. It was hard, slow work. The new

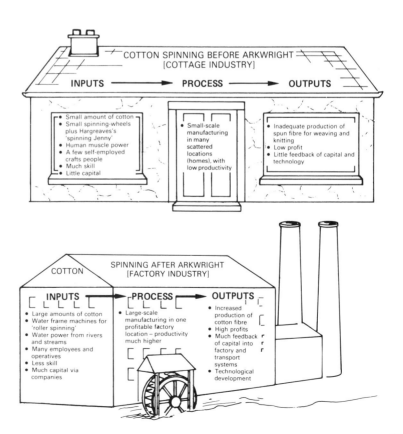

optimal location
The place which an entrepreneur considers most suitable for the siting of an enterprise because it is expected that costs will be lowest there. It is also known as the *least-cost location*.

fibre, cotton, was grown cheaply in Britain's colonies, but not enough yarn could be produced to keep the knitters and weavers supplied. There was a rapidly expanding market for cloth. Richard Arkwright is significant because he saw far beyond the invention of his water frame. His mill and industrial village at Cromford pointed the way to a new industrial system based on **optimal locations**. The first Industrial Revolution and its factory system were to change the face of much of the East Midlands and Great Britain within a hundred years (Fig. 7.1).

Find out all you can about the location of the first factories in your area.

Least-cost location – the Corby story

Many geography texts have used the iron and steel industry to explain industrial systems and the principles of industrial location. What are the factors that influence the growth and decline of an industry in a particular place? Corby's story as a steel town illustrates the system and the factors.

By 1900 the iron industry had spread from Derbyshire to the Scunthorpe area of Lincolnshire (now in Humberside) and to Northamptonshire. Though iron ore was quarried around Corby in 1882, soon after the Midland Railway cut through the area, blast furnaces were not sited there until 1910. It was another 30 years before steelmaking was fully established at Corby. Table 7.1 shows how the two World Wars stimulated investment, employment and production. The town grew rapidly, with thousands of workers moving to Corby from older steel areas in Scotland in search of a more secure future. Industrial entrepreneurs will consider all or some

Table 7.1 *The rise of Corby as a steel town*

Year	Blast furnaces	Steel converters	Production (tonnes)		Employees	Corby population
			Pig-iron	Steel		
1914	2	–	50,000	–	650	1,350
1939	4	3	565,000	498,000	3,950	10,900
1950	4	7	650,000	724,000	7,750	15,700
1960	4	9	895,000	1,147,500	14,000	35,000

Source: D. C. D. Pocock, *East Midland Geographer* **15**, 1961.

Table 7.2 *Principles of industrial location*

- Cost of raw materials or components
- Size of accessible market (area in which output is sold)
- Energy costs
- Cost of workforce with appropriate skills
- Reliability of workforce (competition for skills, labour relations)
- Transport costs (time–distance factors relating to the market area)
- Capital costs, including public grants or subsidies available locally
- Site costs, including subsidies for purchase, leasing and rates
- Access to local research and development facilities, e.g. a university or science park
- Attractiveness of area to key employees

of the factors shown in Table 7.2 when seeking their least-cost locations.

> Choose any manufacturing industry in your area, or one that you know well. Referring to Table 7.2, draw diagrams to illustrate its process(es) and the reasons for its location.

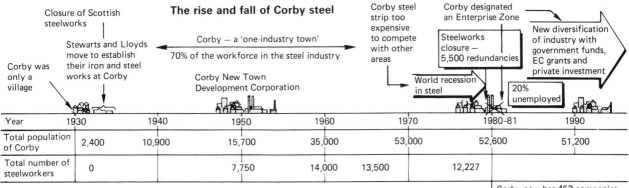

Fig. 7.2. *The rise and fall of Corby steel.*

The Corby story (Fig. 7.2) shows very clearly how the factors of industrial location can work for or against a particular area in a very short time. It also demonstrates that political beliefs and government policies have become major factors since 1945. The Labour government of 1945 to 1951 applied the ideas of state ownership and nationalisation to what it saw as the key sectors of British industry, including coal and steel. Since then central and local government have tried to assist economic growth in particular areas. Corby and Northampton are examples in the region.

Northampton-promoted developments.

NORTHAMPTON IS AN IDEAL LOCATION FOR NATIONAL DISTRIBUTION

Northampton is located halfway between London and Birmingham, Oxford and Cambridge, Southampton and Harwich, and has first class road and rail links to most of Britain's industrial and commercial centres.

And easy access onwards into Europe and more distant international markets.

When Northampton expanded dramatically in the 19th century, its wealth was centred on the boot and shoemaking industry.

Today's expansion is far more broadly based, and it is both industrial and commercial. Most of the factories and warehouses are in the new employment areas, with many of the offices in or near the town centre.

The town's stable and varied workforce of some 90,000 has one of the best records on industrial relations in the UK.

primary industry
An economic activity based on natural resources and products. Includes farming, forestry and fishing, mining and quarrying.

secondary industry
Includes all kinds of manufacturing and has several sub-divisions: e.g. heavy industry using large quantities of raw materials and having bulky products; light or assembly industries usually based on components from elsewhere; footloose industries which can be located almost anywhere.

tertiary sector
Consists of services and has many sub-divisions: e.g. wholesaling and retailing of goods; transport; financial and professional services; public services including government, education, security, and defence.

Reflecting in 1991 on the 1987 view of the 'new industrial revolution', Rolls-Royce spokesman, Ian Charteris, said:

Many companies went out of business either because they failed to change their product to suit new markets, or because they lacked the foresight to modernise their manufacturing techniques and thus became uncompetitive. Rolls-Royce, however, has long lived in the high-tech world of aero engines. Accustomed to continued technical change and fierce competition, it set about streamlining not only its equipment but also its organisation and its production techniques.

Inevitably machines replaced workers. Rolls-Royce now employs around 14,000 but has retained its place as a major international aero-engine manufacturer. The company is now joined in Derby by the Japanese car maker, Toyota, both typifying successful technology-driven firms in the manufacturing sector. Technology has also created an upsurge in many new, smaller firms providing employment in light engineering, computers and the leisure industry.

Fig. 7.3. *Fall and rise of Derby*.
Source: Derby Evening Telegraph, January 1988.

In the 1980s, Conservative governments rejected state ownership and began to privatise publicly owned industries. However, despite changes of governments and policies, there has been one consistent industrial trend since 1945: employment in **primary** and **secondary industries** has declined. The **tertiary sector** has become the major source of jobs. This applies in the East Midlands and the UK, and in most industrial nations.

The fall and rise of Derby

We can learn more about industrial location and changing employment patterns from Derby. In 1987 the *Derby Evening Telegraph* published a special report on a 'new industrial revolution' (Fig. 7.3). These extracts show that despite its very different location and history, the same trends are found in Derby.

The fall and rise of a city – out of ashes spring hope

● Derby has seen a new industrial revolution in the past 20 years – a dramatic change in business after mass redundancies. Traditional heavy industry has taken a battering, and a new breed of high-tech business is now making its mark. In this special report, John Coppock investigates how industry, in the city, has changed over two decades.

It was 1968 and Britain was booming. Heavy industry in Derby reached new heights of success and business had never been better for many traditional firms. Twenty years later, the bottom has fallen out of many traditional markets and the demise of heavy industry has meant unemployment is rife. But Britain is beginning to boom again, after an industrial revolution that has changed the face of the city.

In 1968 Derby was dominated by three main industries. Rolls-Royce, the giant aero-engines firm, employed a staggering 27,000 people, while British Rail Engineering Ltd – then called British Rail Workshops – employed 7,000 and Courtaulds Acetate – formerly British Celanese – employed around 6,500 workers. Together the 'Big Three' employed around a half of the available workforce, and other heavy industry also had thousands of workers. But in the last 20 years more than 20,000 jobs have been shed by the big three alone and many other firms have gone bust.

The recession of the 1970s and early 1980s, massive inflation and the huge 1973 oil price rise led to thousands of redundancies. But the main cause of unemployment has been blamed on new technology which has replaced men with machines. Rolls-Royce's complex aero-engines business thrived on technological advances, but the traditional Derbyshire textile industry was devastated by new technological advances and, ironically, by synthetic products.

But it was also the upsurge in new technology that led to a new industrial base. The result was a shift in industrial emphasis over 20 years and the creation of new jobs in high-tech and leisure industries.

Look carefully at the analysis of economic changes in Derby presented in Fig. 7.3. Draft a special report for a local newspaper article on changing unemployment in any town that you know well.

The end of Players at Radford.

Changing jobs in Nottingham?

Nottingham, the region's largest centre, has also felt the impact of industrial change. The city enjoyed the security of a broad industrial base for over a century. Between 1880 and 1914, big new companies grew up alongside the older textile factories. Household names like Boots, Players and Raleigh date from this period. At their peak, the big firms, later including Plessey, employed over 30,000 people. In 1971 the tobacco industry in Nottingham employed 7,500 workers. However, 1971 and 1981 census data (Table 7.3) point to the same trends as are seen in Derby. Behind these statistics are changes to whole neighbourhoods where families often worked in the same factory through several generations. Radford, where the massive Players factory was demolished in 1987, is an **inner city area** with many jobless and serious social problems. However, in most parts of the region the growth of tertiary work and new secondary industry has kept unemployment below the national average. Data from Northamptonshire, the county nearest to the rapidly expanding economy of the south-east of England, illustrate this (Figs 7.4, 7.5).

Table 7.3 *Greater Nottingham, percentage change in manufacturing jobs, 1971–81*

Textiles	− 50
Clothing	− 27
Food, drink, tobacco	− 25
Vehicles (incl. Raleigh)	− 20
Mechanical engineering (incl. Plessey)	− 26
Timber & furniture	− 29
Paper & printing	− 15
Chemicals (incl. Boots)	+ 6

Source: Census data.

inner city area
An area close to a city centre with many large, old houses in poor condition. These provide cheap accommodation for low-income groups who are often unable to find anything better. Many immigrants went to such areas when they first arrived in Britain, and concentrations of ethnic minorities are characteristic of inner city areas.

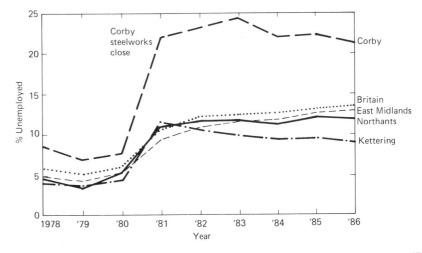

Fig. 7.4. *Local, regional and national unemployment trends, 1978–86.*
Source: Northamptonshire County Council.

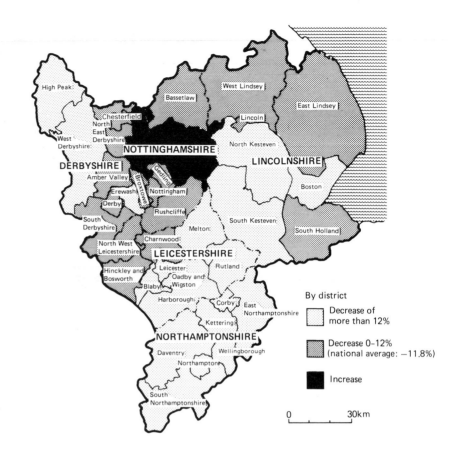

Fig. 7.5. *Changes in unemployment levels, 1986–87.*
Source: Derbyshire County Council

Even here, with the collapse of its steel industry the Corby area has had unemployment problems for several years. Despite investment by central and local government we can see that the problem has persisted through the 1980s in this part of Northamptonshire. This indicates the difficulty of creating industrial growth in some areas. Data from Nottingham and Derby illustrate the problems in very different geographical conditions. An extract from the *1987 City of Nottingham Local Plan* details the difficulties in the region's largest centre.

> Despite the recession the City of Nottingham remains a major centre of employment. In 1976 there were approximately 144,900 jobs in Nottingham, and this had increased to over 150,000 by 1981. A large number of these jobs were filled by people living outside the City, however, and unemployment in the City is high. The number of unemployed people in Nottingham rose from some 6,000 in 1971 to around 15,200 in 1981 and over 23,000 by December 1986. The unemployment rate varies considerably in different parts of Nottingham. In some areas of the inner city it is estimated that over 50% of the working population are without a job.
>
> Some sections of the community, including black people, people with disabilities, the low-skilled and school leavers, are affected particularly seriously by unemployment. Many women work in low-skilled and poor-paying occupations, which have been increasingly subject to employment decline. If all the various needs of unemployed people are to be met . . . a range of training initiatives . . . will be particularly important.

Fig. 7.6. Derby – *distribution of unemployment, 1985.*(left)
Source: Derby City Council Planning Department.

1 List the groups particularly affected by unemployment in Nottingham and in any area you know well. Why are people in such groups more often unemployed?
2 Find out all you can about schemes designed to help them to find new jobs. You might try to talk to people who have experience of such schemes.

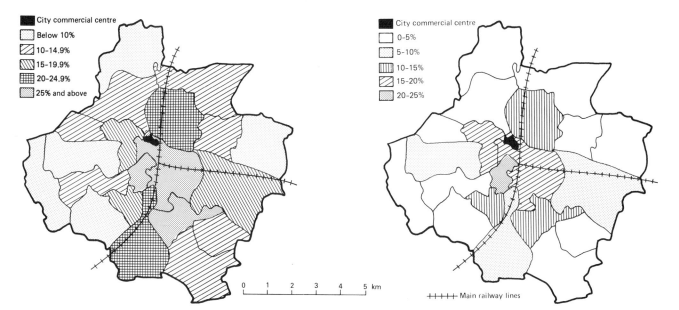

Fig. 7.7. Derby – *households without bath and indoor WC, 1981.* (right)
Source: Derby City Council Planning Department.

visual correlation
In statistics, a correlation measures the link or connection between two data sets or distributions of values. For example, we would expect to find a general connection between measures of height and weight across a large number of people or a population. In geography it is often useful to graph or map data and to look for a visual connection or correlation between the patterns – as in Figs. 7.6 and 7.7. However, a correlation does not *prove* that one set or distribution has caused the other.

urban deprivation
People are said to be deprived when they lack many of the basics, e.g. housing, jobs, diet, which are accepted to be the norm for most others in a society. Deprived groups are typical of inner city areas – hence the term urban deprivation.

Mapping unemployment data in another major town produces clear patterns (Fig. 7.6). If the map of low-quality housing is added we can see similar patterns (Fig. 7.7). That is, in Derby the areas of high unemployment coincide to a large extent with those that have poor housing conditions. In geography we often call this connection between patterns a **visual correlation**. These poor living conditions in the towns and cities are described as **urban deprivation**.

Encouraging enterprise and employment

We have seen in this chapter that there have been major changes in employment patterns in the East Midlands since 1970. These reflect national and international trends. Investigating changing employment patterns in the region led us to similar patterns of poverty and deprivation, especially in some urban areas. We know, however, that a correlation does not *prove* that one pattern causes another.

It is difficult to explain patterns like unemployment and poverty. It is even harder to get agreement on how to solve the problems they represent. All recent governments, however, have agreed on the need to invest in improving the conditions for new economic activities. All saw that changes in technology and markets would lead to changes in industrial types and locations. It was clear that Britain's reliance on heavy industries would be reduced. Industrial location on or near coalfields and ports would be less important. Many new industries would depend more on the skills and enterprise of the workers and managers.

Manpower Services Commission (MSC)

The MSC was set up in 1974 by the Employment and Training Act to run government-funded training services. Its purpose was to improve the quality of Britain's workforce and to help individuals to become more employable as work patterns changed. In 1989 it was re-named the Training Agency, and then from 1990 continued its work as part of the Department of Employment.

Fig. 7.8. *Government support for occupational changes and economic growth, 1970s and 1980s.*
Source: Central Statisical Office.

The **Manpower Services Commission (MSC)**, established in 1974, was one of the main methods used by governments to assist new developments in all industrial sectors. The dramatic rise in unemployment led to many other government initiatives alongside the MSC in the 1980s (Fig. 7.8 and Table 7.4).

Table 7.4 *Government expenditure on regional assistance to industry, 1986–87*

	£ (millions)	Percentage of expenditure in Great Britain
Scotland	241.6	32.9
Wales	144.0	19.6
North	137.1	18.6
North West	128.5	17.5
Yorks & Humberside	41.4	5.6
South West	22.2	3.0
East Midlands	*10.5*	*1.4*
West Midlands	10.0	1.4
Great Britain	735.3	100.0

Source: Central Statistical Office.

---

1 Describe and try to explain the distribution of government aid to industry (Table 7.4).
2 Find out all you can about training and enterprise allowance schemes in your area. Try to talk to people who have first-hand experience of such schemes.

Summary

- We can think of the region's manufacturing industries as systems designed to produce goods for maximum profit. In parts of the East Midlands factory systems altered the environment and ways of life.

- Manufacturers make decisions about the best locations for their factories. Industries and their locations have changed greatly in the region since 1945 as technology has developed and markets have altered. Government policies have also been important.

- Employment in manufacturing has fallen nationally since the war. There has been a large increase in jobs in the tertiary sector.

- Unemployment rose nationally from the mid-1970s to the mid-1980s and again in the early 1990s. The rate in the East Midlands was below the national average, but there are persistent concentrations in some areas.

- Unemployment is strongly correlated with poverty and urban deprivation in some parts of the region. These are seen as serious problems by central and local government. There has been large investment by both to try to solve these problems. However, there are conflicting political views about causes and solutions.

8 Central places and rural spaces

Place and function

We saw in Chapter 2 that the patterns of settlement in the East Midlands have developed over a long period. In geography we try to explain the size and spacing of places. One simple approach is to classify settlements according to where they were established and why. For example, Lincoln is sited where the River Witham cuts through the Lincoln Edge. Its location was obviously important for transport and defence. Boston, the region's principal port, is at the lowest bridging point on the Witham. Such a classification reminds us of the wide range of settlement conditions in the region.

(a) Copy and complete the following table:

	Site and location	Original function
Boston	Lowest bridging point	Port and market
Buxton		
Coalville		
Matlock		
Newark		
Oakham		
Skegness		
Towcester		

(b) Write a paragraph criticising this simple classification of settlements in the region.

It is clear that modern settlements have a range of functions. The original factors of location may no longer be important in terms of what happens there now. We can get some idea of modern functions by investigating employment patterns. Census data for 1981 allow us to do this for a wide range of urbanised areas in the region (Table 8.1).

Referring to Table 8.1 and using your personal knowledge of places in the region, put the settlements into functional groups.

Selling the services and competing centres

urban field
The area surrounding a centre which it serves and influences. It is also known as the settlement's *sphere of influence* or *hinterland*.

The size and location of many settlements in the region are related to the services they offer to the areas around them. Geographers call these areas **urban fields**. Various methods have been used to plot urban fields.

Table 8.1 *East Midlands: occupations in urban areas, 1981*

	Population	Occupations – % employees in			
		Agriculture and forestry	Energy production and water supply	Manufacturing industries	Service industries
Derbyshire					
Glossop	30,040	0.8	1.8	37.1	51.9
Long Eaton	42,494	0.1	2.6	43.5	48.6
Matlock	13,867	1.5	2.4	26.9	63.2
Swadlincote	33,739	0.6	21.3	36.1	35.5
Leicestershire					
Hinckley	35,611	0.6	3.8	50.6	39.0
Loughborough	46,122	0.4	1.0	44.4	38.8
Melton Mowbray	23,592	1.1	0.8	36.9	56.2
Market Harborough	15,966	2.5	1.0	38.4	41.3
Lincolnshire					
Gainsborough	20,592	0.9	5.4	35.4	50.6
Grantham	31,095	0.8	1.6	35.8	54.6
Louth	13,304	1.7	1.7	22.1	62.4
Spalding	21,699	11.4	1.7	19.5	61.0
Northamptonshire					
Daventry	16,193	0.9	0.9	48.0	42.7
Kettering	45,389	0.4	1.3	37.9	52.3
Oundle	3,283	1.4	5.0	17.3	69.7
Wellingborough	38,772	0.3	0.6	43.3	48.7
Nottinghamshire					
East Retford	19,380	1.5	12.9	24.6	52.5
Southwell	6,404	5.0	8.5	15.4	64.2
Sutton in Ashfield	39,622	0.2	18.1	41.5	33.0
Worksop	34,993	0.6	14.0	27.4	50.7

Note: Data apply to *urban area*, not local government unit; not all categories of employment are included; columns do not add up to 100 per cent.

Source: Central Statistical Office.

Central Place Theory
The best-known theory was the work of a German geographer, Walter Christaller. He saw settlements as 'central places' existing to supply goods and services to surrounding areas. He divided services or functions into different orders or levels of importance. He argued that, given an area with no physical obstacles, urban fields would form circles, which result in hexagonal or six-sided patterns.

Companies and planners often need to know to what extent people are attracted to particular places. The importance of settlements as service centres led to what geographers call **Central Place Theory**. This attempts to explain the size and spacing of all the settlements in a given area. It is based on the useful idea of different levels or orders of services provided by settlements of different sizes. These services or functions range from low-order or convenience goods like those of a village shop, to higher-order, specialist services such as jewellers. Only the larger towns and cities provide the higher-order services, which need larger urban fields to stay in business. Therefore major retail chains study spheres of influence carefully before opening new branches. The spread of branches of Next, which has its head office near Leicester, was a good example of central place theory at work in the 1980s.

Though different orders of functions can be seen in the East Midlands, the reality of competing centres is much more complicated than Christaller's simple geometric patterns.

> Choose any area you know well that contains several central places. Try to estimate their orders and approximate catchments.

Central services and CBDs

In the centres of the region's larger settlements we can see distinct areas in which services are concentrated. These are known as **Central Business Districts (CBDs)**. They are well illustrated by Nottingham and Leicester. In 1971 Nottingham ranked ninth in the UK in terms of sales of 'shopping goods'. These are the higher-order goods and do not include everyday purchases of convenience goods.

The CBD of any city has certain distinct features. Leicester is a good example. A detailed land use map shows the concentration of shops, offices and public buildings (Fig. 8.1). We can also see that the CBD is now partly bounded by inner relief roads and underpasses. Leicester also shows the concentration or clustering of certain types of retail

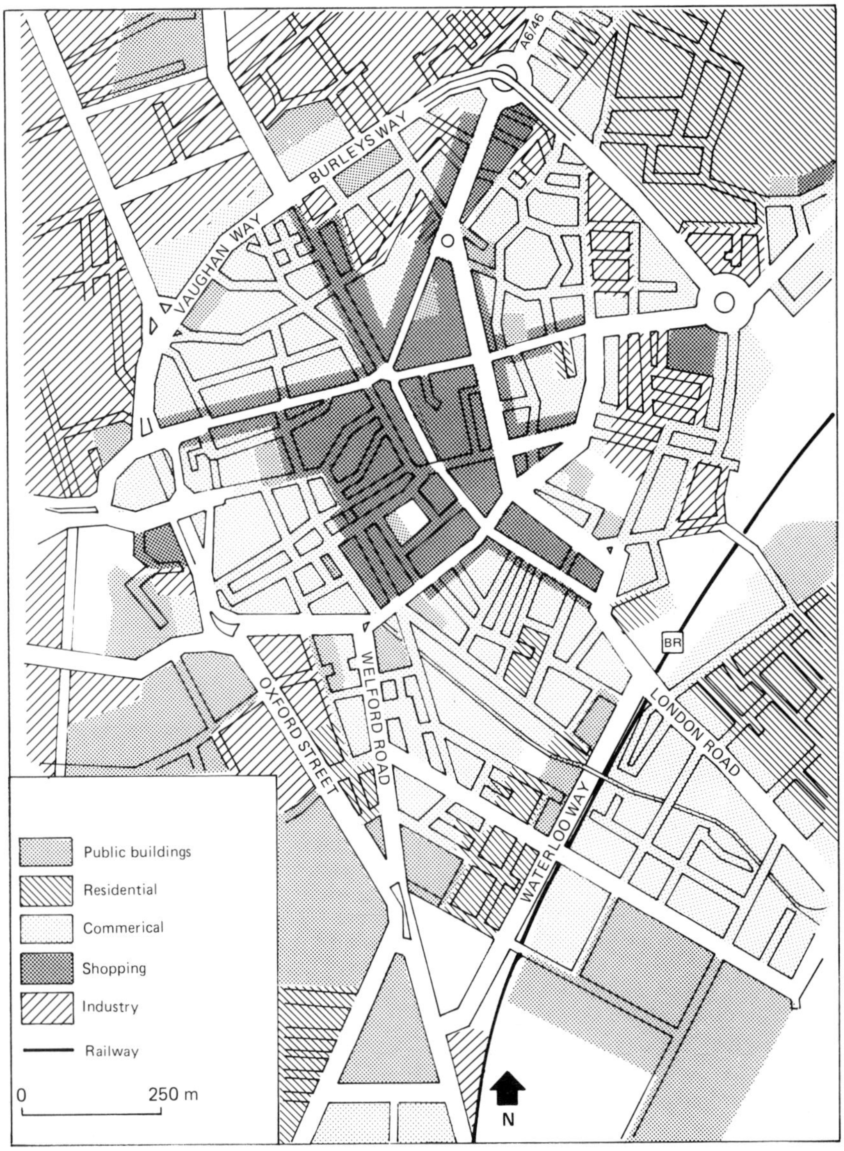

Central Business District
The centre of a city or large town contains concentrations of shops, offices and public buildings. These form the commercial and social core of the settlement.

Fig. 8.1. *Leicester – central area land use.*
Source: Leicester City Council Planning Department.

Fig. 8.2. *Leicester city centre – retail floor space.* (left)
Source: Leicester City Council Planning Department.

Fig. 8.3. *Pedestrian flows in central Leicester.* (right)
Source: Leicester City Council Planning Department.

outlets in the CBD (Fig. 8.2).

The cost of trading in a CBD is much higher than in less central locations. Department and other stores offering higher-order goods must attract from a large urban field. Clustering increases the chances of customers entering a particular higher-order store as they 'shop around'. The movement of people within a CBD also tends to form a distinct pattern. This can be seen in Leicester: surveys of pedestrians show that numbers decline rapidly away from the heart of the CBD, where rents and rates are very high (Fig. 8.3).

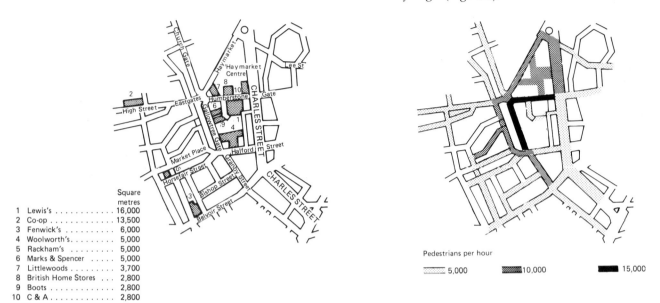

		Square metres
1	Lewis's	16,000
2	Co-op	13,500
3	Fenwick's	6,000
4	Woolworth's	5,000
5	Rackham's	5,000
6	Marks & Spencer	5,000
7	Littlewoods	3,700
8	British Home Stores	2,800
9	Boots	2,800
10	C & A	2,800

Pedestrians per hour: 5,000 / 10,000 / 15,000

superstore
Based on the supermarket idea, superstores sell a wide range of other goods as well as food, e.g. clothing, household and electrical items. They are often sited on the edges of larger urban areas and surrounded by large car parks.

Choose any town or city where you shop regularly. Draw a sketch-map of the main types of land use in its central area. Mark on any 'clustering' of higher-order services and the streets with the greatest pedestrian flows. Try to mark on the boundary of the CBD. Add notes explaining how you did this.

Because of high costs and parking problems in CBDs, cities like Leicester have a complex pattern of service facilities. During the 1980s many district shopping centres were re-developed. **Superstores** such as Asda, the Co-op and Woolco appeared on the city outskirts where large, free parking areas can be provided cheaply.

Blueprint for a shopping dream

Plans for Northampton's huge 26 acre shopping and leisure complex – St James Retail Park – consist of two neighbouring sites between St Peter's Way and the River Nene Access. The multi-million-pound project could create more than 500 jobs.

The developers' plans include:
• A Toys R Us store with 60,000 square feet of floorspace
• A Courts furniture store (45,000 square feet)
• A W. H. Smith DIY store (40,000 square feet).

But the centrepiece of the Citygrove scheme is the mirrored glass 'leisure unit' to be run by Granada, which includes a multiscreen cinema, a café bar, restaurants, mooring facilities for boats, picnic sites along the river bank and parking for 750 cars.

The adjoining site is being developed by B & Q with each store filled with a different branch of their retail empire.

The trend towards multipurpose trading complexes can be seen at St James Retail Park development, in Northampton.
Source: *Chronicle & Echo* (Northampton).

The CBD is the most central of various distinct urban zones. These zones are related to the function and age of buildings, the transport system and the main physical features. Derby can be seen to have a definite **urban structure** when its land use and age of buildings are mapped (Fig. 8.4).

urban structure
As settlements grow, they tend to divide into areas or zones with different functions, e.g. housing, shopping, industry, transport, etc. The pattern formed by these different land uses is called the urban structure.

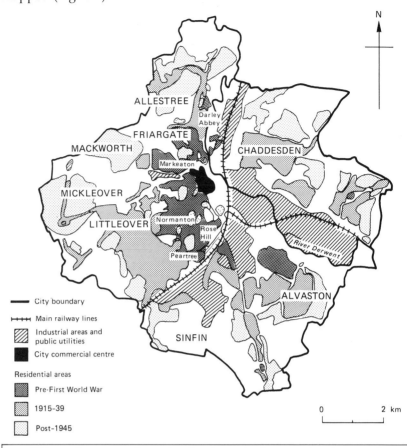

Fig. 8.4. *Urban structure of Derby, 1985.*
Source: Derby City Council Planning Department.

1 Write a short report for a city planning committee, putting the case for and against the development of a large retail/leisure complex on the edge of its urban area.
2 Briefly describe the urban structure of Derby (see Fig. 8.4). Compare it with that of your own town or one that you know well. Can you see any general pattern of urban structure in Derby?

Cores, frames and renewal

Nottingham, the region's largest settlement, tells us more about urban structures. Fig. 8.5 illustrates the idea of the CBD 'core' and its surrounding 'frame'. We can see that the frame contains more varied land use, including hospitals, warehouses, industrial and education buildings. That is, the functions and land values here are different from those at the commercial heart of the city. It is also clear that there have been many changes in Nottingham.

Since about 1960 the centres of most towns and cities in the East Midlands have been re-developed (Tables 8.2, 8.3). Old property has been cleared; new, wider roads and car parks have appeared. This suggests that increasing car ownership is a major factor in modern **urban renewal**.

urban renewal
Inner-city areas of towns and cities can become very decayed. Urban renewal is the term used for a variety of programmes, usually started by public authorities, to systematically remodel and repair such areas.

Fig. 8.5. *Nottingham – core and frame structure, 1965 and 1983.*
Source: Article by J. Giggs in *A New Geography of Nottingham*, Trent Polytechnic 1988.

Table 8.2 *Central Nottingham – land use changes, 1948–83* (floorspace in square metres by major users)

Land use categories	1948 1,000 m²	%	1983 1,000 m²	%	1948–83 (% change)
1 Industry	311.2	24.3	243.7	12.6	– 21.7
2 Warehouse, wholesale	190.4	14.8	157.0	8.1	– 17.5
3 Transport	78.1	6.1	104.5	5.4	+ 33.8
4 Government offices	86.1	6.7	164.3	8.5	+ 90.8
5 Social*	71.4	5.6	203.6	10.5	+ 185.2
6 Entertainment	66.3	5.2	26.9	6.5	+ 91.4
7 Hotels	76.2	5.9	95.6	4.9	+ 25.5
8 Retailing	223.3	17.4	376.5	19.4	+ 68.6
9 Commercial offices	179.8	14.0	467.7	24.1	+ 160.1
Total	1,282.8	100.0	1,839.8	100.0	+ 51.2

*includes education, hospitals, libraries, museums
Source: Brazier *et al. A New Geography of Nottingham*, Trent Polytechnic 1988.

Table 8.3 *Nottingham city centre functions, 1989*

Government buildings	Civic buildings including Shire Hall and Council House, City and County Courts; central fire and police stations; Head Post Office and Counter Services Management
Social welfare/Education	Trent Polytechnic (City site); People's College of Further Education; General Hospital; County Library Central Services; castle and other civic museums, e.g. Costume annd Canal
Recreation/Entertainment	Albert Hall (renovated); Nottingham Playhouse; Royal Concert Hall; major commercial cinemas; Nottingham Film Theatre; Nottingham Theatre Club (Lace Market Theatre); Lace Centre; Ice Stadium; Radios Nottingham and Trent; BBC East Midlands Studios; night clubs
Hotels (major)	Albany and Royal
Retailing	Broad Marsh and Victoria Centres; specialist and department stores
Transport	Broad Marsh and Victoria bus stations

Look carefully at Fig. 8.5 and Tables 8.2, 8.3.
1 Choose any city or sizeable town you know or often visit. Write a short account, and include maps and tables, to show how the core and frame areas have changed since the 1960s. Attempt to explain these changes.
2 Try to express your own feelings about the new 'townscape' in words and drawings. How might a visitor interested in the quality of urban renewal (Prince Charles, say) comment on what he or she would see?

Inside the inner city

We saw in Chapter 7 that there are correlations between the distribution of poverty and unemployment in many inner-city areas. In the 1980s there have been serious problems, including riots, in some of them. In recent years central and local government have made major efforts to overcome the problems of inner cities. Data from Leicester City Council illustrate some correlations, and the problems they represent (Figs. 8.6a–e).

What is the Inner Area?

Roughly speaking, the ring of buildings around the city centre constructed before the First World War . . . the houses, shops and factories are old [and] built to a high density, with narrow roads and small gardens . . . they are often in need of repairs and modernisation . . . Those with less choice move to older housing . . . in the inner area . . . Many such people are more likely to suffer from problems of unemployment, poor health, etc . . .

Leicester City Council is particularly keen on supporting and encouraging voluntary groups both to set up projects and then run them themselves . . . But progress is slow. The amount of money available to

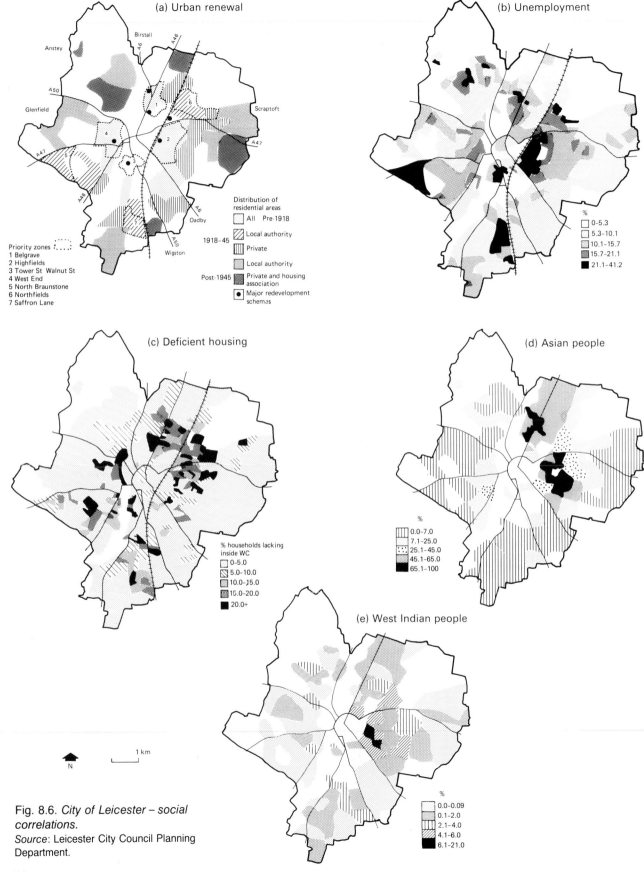

Fig. 8.6. *City of Leicester – social correlations.*
Source: Leicester City Council Planning Department.

the City and County Councils is very small, and does not go the whole way to making up for the absence of private investment which is still attracted to the . . . sites on the edges of the City where inner area problems don't exist.

> Using the above, and drawing on your own experience, draft an article for a city newspaper entitled 'Solving the Problems of the Inner City'. Include reports of interviews with local residents, councillors, police, doctors and business people.

Rural problems

Changes in agricultural employment and transport systems have also led to problems of deprivation in many rural settlements. We know that the distribution of population in the East Midlands is uneven. The major central places are found in the west of the region. Lincolnshire is the largest and least densely populated of the five counties. Leicestershire and Northamptonshire also have large rural areas with scattered settlement patterns. Providing adequate services for such areas has become a major financial problem for local and public authorities. Maps based on a report presented to Leicestershire County Council in 1982 show this clearly (Fig. 8.7).

Fig. 8.7. *Leicestershire rural services in the early 1980s.*
Source: Leicester City Council Planning Department.

Shrinking services in the rural areas

The pattern of schools and colleges shows the same problem. The closure of village primary schools reflects the fall in population in some rural areas. Providing secondary school and college education is also very difficult when pupils' homes are very scattered. Data on telephone boxes reflect the same situation (Fig. 8.8). However, in 1986, British Telecom became a private company, and it must be profitable, so the problem of paying for essential services in rural areas seems likely to become more complex in the future.

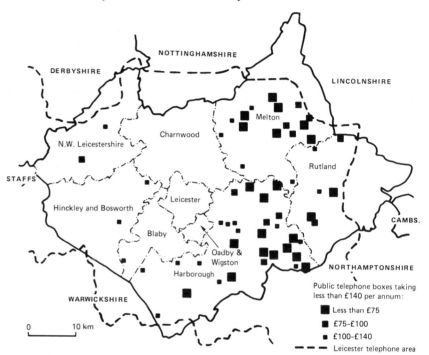

Fig. 8.8. *Uneconomic public telephone kiosks in the Leicester telephone area.*
Source: Leicester City Council Planning Department.

> Referring to Figs. 8.7 and 8.8, and drawing on your own experience of rural areas, draft a short article for a country newspaper under the headline 'Country People are Deprived Too'.

Summary

- Classifying the sites and functions of places helps to explain the development of settlement patterns in the East Midlands.
- The pattern of settlements is related to the services they offer and the areas surrounding them. Central Place Theory is useful in investigating how places are related, and in explaining the hierarchy of settlements in the region.
- The larger centres in the East Midlands have distinct zones or patterns of land use. Urban land use models help to explain these, the problems associated with inner-city areas, and attempts to solve them by urban renewal.
- The East Midlands also has rural areas where changes in population and economic conditions have led to problems of public service provision.

9 Land for living and leisure

Between 1981 and 1986 the population of the East Midlands rose by 3.1 per cent. This was well above the national average. It continued a trend that was clear by the 1970s and seems likely to continue in the 1990s. It is estimated that between the years 1986 and 2001 the region's population will increase by a further 7.1 per cent.

However, again there are considerable variations within the region. We know that people have been leaving the centres of the cities and some rural areas. Other areas are attracting new residents. Figures 9.1 and 9.2 show that Northamptonshire's population has grown rapidly through two decades. People were moving to the county from most other regions in the mid-1980s.

These population trends mean that in many parts of the East Midlands there is considerable pressure on the space available for housing and recreation. In this chapter we will examine some of the responses to this pressure in different parts of the region.

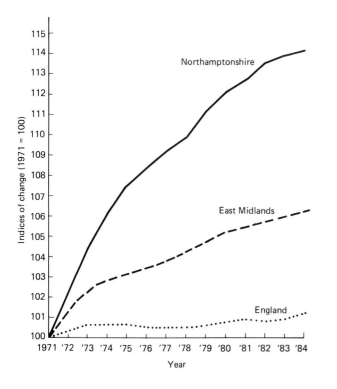

Fig. 9.1. *Northamptonshire population change, 1971–84.* (left)
Source: Northamptonshire County Council Planning Department.

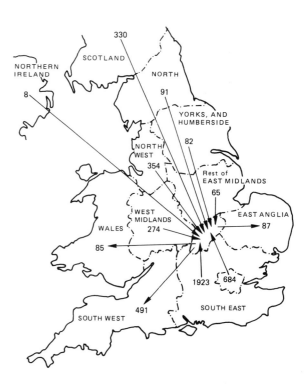

Fig. 9.2. *Northamptonshire net migration flows, 1984.* (right)
Source: Northamptonshire County Council Planning Department.

---

1 Describe the pattern of regional movement to and from Northamptonshire in 1984. Try to explain the main differences.
2 What evidence can you find for population changes in your area?

Table 9.1 *Price of dwellings in the UK, 1981–86*

	Index of dwelling prices (1980 = 100)			Building society borrowers average dwelling price, 1986 (£)	
	1981	1985	1986	All	First-time buyers
United Kingdom	106	144	164	36,300	27,400
North	107	135	146	24,300	18,200
Yorkshire & Humberside	112	143	156	25,600	19,300
East Midlands	108	145	161	28,500	21,400
East Anglia	105	147	171	36,100	28,100
South East				50,400	39,200
Greater London	103	156	190	54,900	45,200
Rest of South East	105	150	176	48,500	35,800
South West	103	140	161	38,500	29,100
West Midlands	104	129	141	28,400	20,700
North West	106	133	146	27,500	20,400
England	105	144	166	37,600	28,500
Wales	109	141	150	27,400	21,100
Scotland	109	147	155	28,200	22,100
Northern Ireland	97	121	129	25,700	21,200

Source: Central Statistical Office.

Raising the roof

Variations in house prices reflect the different pressures on living space. Table 9.1 shows that there were major regional differences in the mid-1980s. A 1988 survey by the Nationwide Anglia Building Society gives valuable detail on the variations within the region. Tables 9.2 and 9.3 show some significant differences in house prices and income of borrowers across the five counties. The data support the corridor-periphery idea discussed in Chapter 2.

> 1 Describe the differences in house prices between the East Midlands counties in 1987–88. How do these differences support the idea of a corridor and periphery pattern of population and economic growth?
> 2 Compare the house price data in Tables 9.1 and 9.2 with current prices in your area. Comment on and try to explain any major changes. Is there evidence of increasing pressure on living space in your area and other parts of the country?
> 3 Find out all you can about the 1988 Housing Act. Ask some local councillors from different parties about their views on it in relation to living space and housing needs in your area.

Living with leisure

There has been a big reduction in working hours in Britain since 1945. During the 1960s the basic 40-hour week was introduced. Leisure time, including paid holidays, has increased considerably. Between 1963 and 1985 the average paid holiday for most full-time manual workers increased from two weeks to four weeks per year. This has led to a rapid growth in the leisure and tourist industries. Tourism was estimated to be Britain's fastest-growing industry in the 1980s,

Table 9.2 *East Midlands – house prices by type, 1987–88* (Nationwide Anglia sales)

	Northants £	Leicestershire £	Lincolnshire £	Derbyshire £	Nottinghamshire £	All buyers £	East Midlands (first-time buyers) £	Female buyers £	UK £
Detached houses	72,712	65,904	57,713	49,595	50,027	58,803	59,737	54,203	80,448
Semi-detached houses	48,422	37,605	35,383	27,337	27,625	34,300	38,937	34,565	52,583
Terraced houses	38,328	27,800	26,939	20,630	21,161	26,656	32,771	24,920	45,549
Bungalows	59,683	58,895	45,186	39,429	39,059	46,109	46,146	47,219	55,885
Flats/maisonettes	36,867	25,217	22,089	18,127	22,610	26,089	32,149	23,572	48,627
Market price, all properties	52,505	43,730	41,515	31,779	31,785	39,496	36,435	33,777	54,668

The average market price of properties bought in the East Midlands at £39,496 was 28 per cent below the average price paid nationally. Within the region average prices ranged from over £50,000 in Northants to just over £30,000 in Derbyshire and Nottinghamshire. Prices in Northants were higher than anywhere else in the region over the whole range of property types and were often on a par with areas much closer to London. Unusually the prices paid by first-time buyers were typically higher than for all buyers for many property types. Overall, however, the prices paid by first-time buyers were lower than for all buyers, as most lending by first-time buyers was at the lower end of the market, in terraced properties, and few expensive detached houses were bought by first-time buyers.

Source: Nationwide Anglia

Table 9.3 East Midlands mortgages – household income of borrowers, 1987–88 (Nationwide Anglia borrowers)

	Northants %	Leicestershire %	Lincolnshire %	Derbyshire %	Nottinghamshire %	All buyers %	East Midlands (first-time buyers) %	Female buyers %	UK %
Household income (weekly)									
Up to and including £100	5	10	9	5	9	7	4	19	6
£101–£150	6	9	11	12	14	11	10	22	7
£151–£200	13	16	18	21	20	18	17	18	13
£201–£250	18	19	21	20	23	20	20	15	16
£251–£300	21	15	16	17	15	17	22	10	15
£301–£350	15	12	10	11	8	11	14	6	12
£350+	22	19	15	14	11	16	13	10	31
Total	100	100	100	100	100	100	100	100	100
Average weekly income (£)	281.91	260.73	246.12	246.97	232.42	252.50	251.51	200.00	302.95
Annual equivalent (£)	14,659	13,558	12,798	12,842	12,086	13,130	13,079	10,400	15,753

The average annual income of Nationwide Anglia borrowers in the East Midlands at £13,130 was 17 per cent below the average for the United Kingdom as a whole (£15,753). Within the region average household incomes ranged from £14,659 in Northants to £12,086 in Nottinghamshire. 23 per cent of borrowers in Nottinghamshire had incomes of £150 a week or less compared with only 11 per cent in Northants. At the other end of the income scale 37 per cent of borrowers in Northants had incomes of £300 a week or more compared with 43 per cent nationally and only 19 per cent in Nottinghamshire. Despite the relatively high proportion of women in clerical/managerial jobs in the East Midlands their incomes typically did not match this status. 41 per cent of women buyers had incomes of £150 a week or less contributing to an annual income of £10,400 (£200 a week), 21 per cent (or over £50 a week) below that for all buyers in the region.

Source: Nationwide Anglia

producing about 50,000 new jobs each year. Various surveys in the 1970s and '80s offer evidence of the rapid growth of leisure activities nationally and in the East Midlands.

We know that the East Midlands contains a great variety of physical environments. This variety is the basis of a wide range of recreational attractions, particularly outdoors. Figure 9.3 shows the region's major areas of natural beauty, open country with public access and recreation sites. It is clear from the map that recreational pressure is concentrated in certain areas within the region.

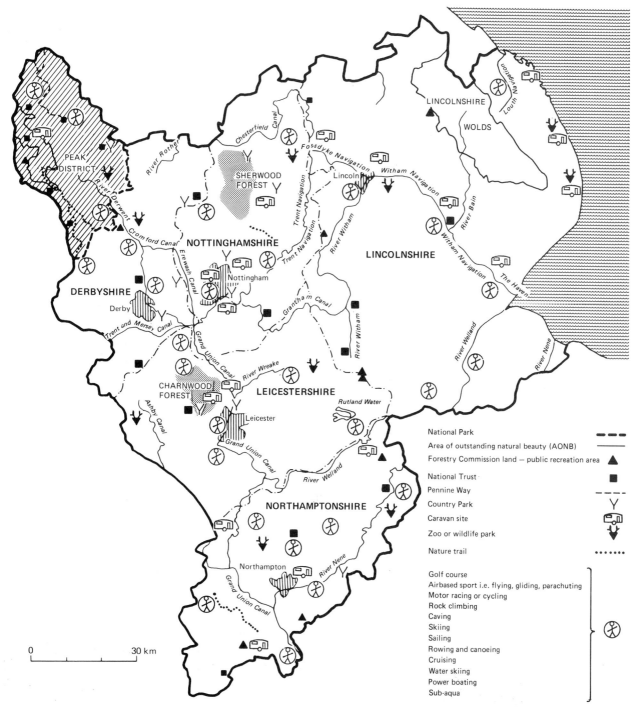

Fig. 9.3. *Recreational environments and facilities in the East Midlands, 1985.*
Source: Based on East Midland Tourist Board data.

Scenery and seaside

The East Midlands has limited seaside space that is easily accessible to all its population. Resorts are restricted to parts of the Lincolnshire coast. Surveys show that the catchment area of this holiday coast is relatively small (Fig. 9.4).

Many British seaside resorts were largely created by the railway age. Skegness, for example, retains a direct rail link with Nottingham and Derby. However, the majority of visitors now travel by road. Also many British resorts now need much modernisation to compete with foreign package holidays. Thus those local authorities trying to develop their tourist industries must attract investment. The relative isolation of the Lincolnshire resorts adds to the difficulties for the East Lindsey authority. (See Table 9.4.)

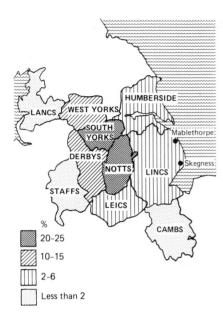

Fig. 9.4. *Skegness and Mablethorpe – staying visitors' catchment by county, 1980.*
Source: *The Lincolnshire Coast Tourism Initiatives Study, 1981* East Lindsey District Council.

Table 9.4 *Skegness – visitors' perceptions of development needs*

	Day trippers		Staying visitors		All visitors	
	No.	%	No.	%	No.	%
Rebuild pier	9,857	25.9	5,370	6.6	15,227	12.8
Better entertainments, e.g. more/better shows, good theatre, more/better discos, cheaper amusements	3,924	10.4	24,505	30.4	28,489	23.8
Sports/leisure facilities, e.g. indoor, heated swimming pool, sports/leisure centre	1,853	4.9	6,001	7.8	7,854	6.6
Wet weather facilities	–	–	1,467	1.8	1,467	1.2
Other facilities/amenities, e.g. more/better toilets, more/better gardens/parks, better shops/supermarkets	3,486	9.2	11,772	14.4	15,258	12.8
Car parking/accessibility, e.g. more/better/cheaper car parking, better bus services	9,371	24.6	7,794	9.7	17,165	14.5
Environmental improvements, e.g. clean the beach, more control of dogs, more litter bins, pedestrianise High Street	5,401	14.1	10,264	12.7	15,665	13.2

Source: East Lindsey District Council Survey, 1980

---

1 Describe the general pattern of recreational facilities in the East Midlands.
2 Imagine you are a tourist industry consultant to the East Lindsey District Council. Using the information in Figs 9.3, 9.4 and Table 9.4, and drawing on your own experience of seaside resorts, draft a short report on the future development of Skegness and Mablethorpe as tourist centres.

Parks, pleasure and protection

We know from Chapter 3 that the East Midlands contains a large part of the first national park set up in England and Wales. The Peak National Park Planning Board is responsible for 'the protection and enhancement of the Park's landscape and the provision for enjoyment of the Park by the public'. Figure 9.5 shows that the Park is surrounded by major areas of population including some in the East Midlands.

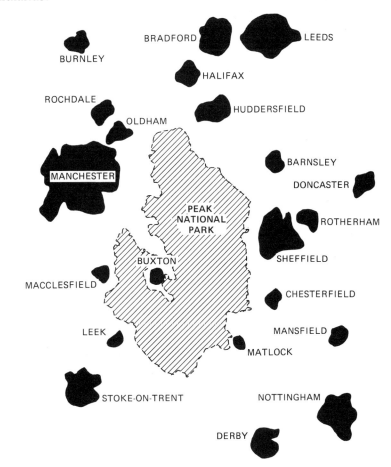

Fig. 9.5. *Regional context of the Peak National Park.*
Source: Peak National Park.

Table 9.5 *Summary of Peak National Park visitor survey, 1986–87*

- There are about 18.5 million visits to the Park each year.
- Over 95% of visitors have been to the Peak district before.
- Regular visitors account for 5 million visits per year.
- 65% of day visitors are from the surrounding conurbations.
- Over 10% of visits to the Peak area are made by staying visitors.
- The holiday season is concentrated within the summer months.
- 80 per cent of holidays are short breaks of less than 7 days.
- Nearly a half of all staying visitors to the Park stay in surrounding towns and villages.
- In summer over half of all visitor-nights are on camping or caravanning holidays.
- Visitors are attracted to the Peak's unspoilt open countryside and to its villages and towns; for example, 60 per cent rate 'uncommercialised areas' as very important.
- The most popular areas for visitors are the Lower Derwent, Wye and Hope Valleys.
- The major recreational activities in the Park are sightseeing and hiking.
- Over 40 per cent of visitors set out to visit a particular area.
- Visitors return to areas they have been to before.
- Each year visitor spending generates over £75 million for the local economy.
- Visitor spending has risen in real terms by 38 per cent between 1971/72 and 1986/87.

By the mid-1970s over 16 million people lived within easy day-trip distance of the Park. This was over one-third of the total population of England and Wales. There were nearly 4 million cars owned in this catchment. Ten years later a visitor survey showed that the Peak landscape was under increasing recreational pressure. The estimated number of visits to the Park each year was approaching 20 million in 1987. This survey illustrates the major economic importance of the leisure industry, and the concentration of visitor pressure in certain areas, particularly in Derbyshire (Table 9.5).

Most outdoor recreation is based on road transport, especially private cars. The survey showed that about 75,000 cars stop on an average Sunday for at least ten minutes in the Park. There may be 25,000 cars parked there at any one time. Providing for this aspect of recreational pressure is very difficult.

It is clear that one of the major problems in this part of the East Midlands is how to balance the need for recreational space with the

Nature Conservancy Council
A government-funded body set up to manage National Nature Reserves, to protect and preserve threatened ecologies, and to advise government under the terms of the 1981 Wildlife and Countryside Act concerning areas of special ecological interest and those at risk. The scope of its activity will probably alter in the 1990s if it is merged with the Countryside Commission (as in Scotland and Wales).

conservation of the area's natural beauty. The **Nature Conservancy Council (NCC)** sets up National Nature Reserves (NNRs) and Sites of Special Scientific Interest (SSSIs) to protect aspects of the environment. The NCC works with the Park Board on conservation matters in the Peak National Park. It has established 54 SSSIs covering 20,000 hectares – about 18 per cent of the Park. The Board assessed the recreational space capacity of the Park in the 1970s. It was found that much of the landscape cannot support intensive recreational use without damaging the environment.

1 Referring to Table 9.5, describe the main attractions and disadvantages of the Peak National Park for:
(a) a retired couple with a car living in Long Eaton;
(b) a couple with two children, a large dog and a caravan living in Ashby;
(c) a motorbike scrambler club in Kettering;
(d) a single mother from Sleaford whose two teenage children are keen on youth hostelling;
(e) a YTS trainee from Worksop whose hobby is cycle road racing.

2 The Whistlestop project (Fig. 9.6) is a combined venture involving a voluntary organisation, a local council and British Rail. What are the advantages and disadvantages of such a scheme in relation to the land use conflict discussed in this chapter? Briefly describe any area where you know such a conflict exists. How would you try to solve the problem?

Table 9.6 *Major tourist attractions in the East Midlands, 1987*

Attraction	Million visitors
Bradgate Park, Leics.	1,200
Clumber Park, Notts.	1,000
Sherwood Forest CP, Notts.	0,900
Billing Aquadrome, Northants.	0,750
Elvaston Castle CP, Derbys.	0,720
Wicksteed CP, Northants.	0,500
Irchester CP, Northants.	0,462
Twycross Zoo, Leics.	0,461
Rutland Water, Leics.	0,460
Nottingham Castle	0,438
American Adventure, Derbys.	0,400
Beacon CP, Leics.	0,350
Upper Derwent Reservoirs, Derbys.	0,250
Barnwell CP, Northants.	0,226
Heights of Abraham, Derbys.	0,201
Lincoln Cathedral	0,200
Wollaton Hall, Nottingham	0,193
Gibraltar Point Nature Res., Lincs.	0,180
Riber Castle Wildlife Park, Derbys.	0,168
Brewhouse Yard Museum, Nottingham	0,160

CP = Country Park
publicly owned and local authorities are

Tourist Top Twenty

The data in Tables 9.6 and 9.7 show clearly how important are the leisure and tourist industries to the region. Many of these attractions are publicly owned, and local authorities are major investors in the region's leisure and tourist industries.
(a) Mark the region's most popular tourist attractions on a map.
(b) Construct a table dividing them into categories and listing the likely reasons for their success.

Table 9.7 *East Midlands tourist industry – spending and employment, 1987–88*

	Tourist spending (£ million, estimated)	Full-time job equivalents (estimate)
Derbyshire	132	9,000
Leicestershire	104	7,250
Lincolnshire	115	8,000
Northamptonshire	94	6,500
Nottinghamshire	105*	7,250

* not including Center Parcs, which is expected to be at least £11 million
Source: East Midlands Tourist Board.

Derbyshire Wildlife Whistlestop Countryside Centre

Derbyshire Wildlife Trust is the county's only voluntary organisation concerned with nature conservation. It has set up 51 nature reserves and over 1,000 acres of the county are now protected in this way.

Understanding and enjoyment both play a vital part in helping to protect our heritage. The more we all understand and enjoy the old buildings, landscape and wildlife around us, the less chance they will be damaged and destroyed.

The Derbyshire Wildlife Trust believes that enjoyment and understanding play a major part in the ultimate conservation of wildlife. Through the co-operation of Derbyshire Dales District Council the Trust now has a unique opportunity to create a Wildlife Information and Education Centre at Matlock Bath Old Railway Station. The Trust proposes to convert the station buildings into the 'Whistlestop Wildlife Centre'. Built in an unusual 'chalet style' these Grade II Historic Listed Buildings reflect Victorian attempts to promote Matlock Bath as England's answer to Switzerland!

Located on the edge of a large car park close to High Tor recreation ground and the Heights of Abraham cable-car, the centre will be ideally situated to bring the wildlife message to large numbers of visitors in this popular resort.

The Trust intends to renovate the buildings completely, bringing them back into first class condition. One will be equipped as a shop, information and exhibition area and the other as a lecture theatre and education centre for visiting schools and other groups. These facilities will therefore provide an important springboard for the public to increase its enjoyment of the Derbyshire countryside.

Successful completion of the project will not only help to encourage the protection of wildlife and facilitate important educational work, but it will simultaneously protect a fascinating piece of Victorian 'Railwayana'. The direct results will be a feature of Derbyshire for generations to come.

Fig. 9.6. *Whistlestop Countryside Centre at Matlock Bath. The need to bring conservation and commercial interests together has produced new recreational and educational ventures in the region. Whistlestop Wildlife Centre at Matlock Bath is a good example.*
Source: Whistlestop Countryside Centre.

Threatened Habitats

Whilst the Trust's new Visitor Centre will be an important contribution to wildlife conservation in general, some places where wildlife lives, such as wildflower rich meadows and pastures, ancient woods, moorland, marsh and waterside places amongst others, are so important that the Trust feels compelled to seek to buy further examples of them outright to ensure their future. This is especially the case when a site is under imminent threat of damage or destruction.

Train Time at the Whistlestop

All manner of trains must have called at Matlock Bath Station since 1849 when the buildings were erected.

Selling Sherwood

Because of the Robin Hood legend, Sherwood Forest is one of the best-known places in the East Midlands. Nottinghamshire County Council has begun to develop its tourist potential, and has encouraged a major private investment alongside the area's older country parks, like the one at Rufford.

Going Dutch – a place for all seasons

Mieke van Nunen has enjoyed her four years as part of the management team at the Center Parcs Holiday Village at Sherwood. She has seen the 180-hectare development take shape and flourish since 1986 when construction began (Fig. 9.7). Mieke points to the 300,000 guests per year who come by car from all over Britain, and to the 100 per cent occupancy of the 709 villas since the opening in July 1987, with obvious pride and satisfaction.

> I think we have brought something quite new to the leisure industry in Britain. It's not easy to find the right words in English to describe our concept properly. It's much more than a short-break holiday. We've been working it out since 1967 in Holland and Belgium. All locations must have a forest setting. None is on the coast, but water is the other key environment feature.

> Piet Derksen, our chairman and founder, has a passionate belief in this. He first saw the commercial potential in an escape environment where trees and water help to shut out the pressures of urban living. It must be to some extent weatherproof. The season must be the whole year and people must be free to choose the sort of recreation best for them.

Mieke is very aware of the company's need to satisfy the balance between economic success and conservation. She knows that the Nottinghamshire local authorities were impressed by this when visiting Center Parcs' Dutch sites before giving planning approval.

> The beauty is, we have to work with nature to protect the basis of our business. We have planted 360,000 trees and shrubs here, transferred water plants from Clumber Park, and sited hundreds of nesting boxes. With our lakes and waterways we are creating a new tree- and water-based ecology. People find it much more attractive than the rather gloomy pinewoods they planted on these dry soils before.

> You know, from the A614 you can't really tell we are here! Yet we employ 400 people and are putting an extra £10 million into the local economy. We provide 7,000 jobs in Europe and have 2.5 million visitors. We must go on developing our ideas in the locations where environment and catchment are right. You cannot stand still in a world where work, leisure and technology are always changing.

Try to identify and justify four possible future locations for Center Parcs in the UK.

Write a supporting document to a planning body for the siting of a holiday village or a venture in the leisure industry that you feel combines good business with sound environmental considerations.

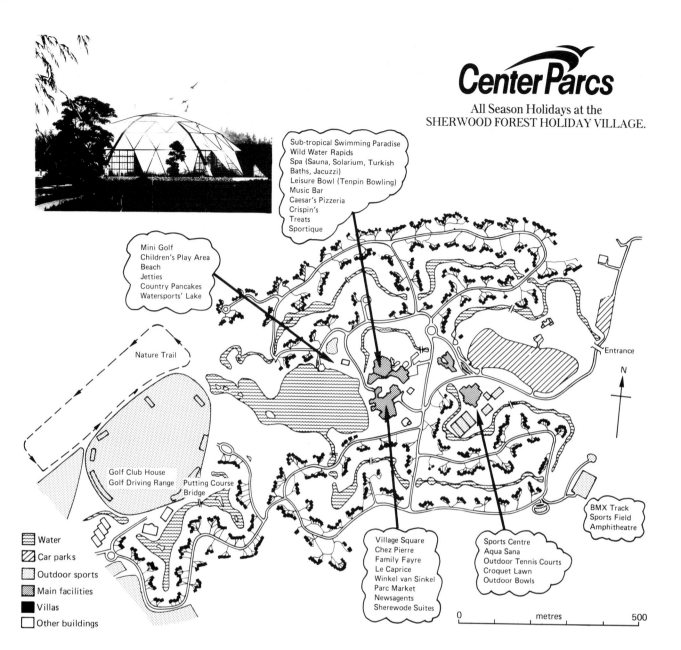

Fig. 9.7. *Center Parcs, Sherwood Forest.*
Source: Center Parcs.

Summary

- The growth of population in the region has been well above the national average in recent years. This has meant increased pressure on the land available for residential use. Again there are significant differences within the East Midlands.

- The demand for recreational space has also increased nationally and within the region. The type and distribution of recreational land use in the East Midlands reflects its variety of environments and its central location as a tourist area.

- The development of different types of recreational resources in the East Midlands illustrates how different interests can conflict or combine over the development of space for living and leisure.

10 A choice of futures – a future of choices?

In *The East Midlands* we have seen that regional geography is a way of looking at landscape and life in a particular area. We found that the region's cultural landscape was the result of many human decisions over many generations. We noted the amazing speed of technological change in recent years, and saw how political and technical developments could modify whole landscapes in a few years. It also means sudden changes in economic systems. These can transform work patterns and lifestyles across whole areas and communities. Many people find these changes very difficult to come to terms with.

The only certainty about the East Midlands is that these changes will continue. They may well become more rapid and harder to understand. One important difference in *our* lifetime is that, by law, more systematic attempts are being made to control and plan changes to our environment. In this last chapter some of the region's planners give us their thoughts on the future issues and choices facing the East Midlands as we approach a new century.

The following are personal views, not official county planning policies. They are brief extracts from longer statements kindly provided by chief planning officers or the chairpersons of planning committees in 1989. Local authority plans can have much influence on the changing face of the region. To what extent do these views of the future from within the region link with our geographical view of its past and present?

DERBYSHIRE County Council
Supports Nuclear Free Zones

Derbyshire lies at a regional frontier, between the Midlands and the North. This has given it a distinctive character of attractive countryside, old-established industrial areas and rich mineral deposits. The dramatic decline in primary and manufacturing employment during the 1980s... will continue with further losses of mining employment during the 1990s and consequent job losses in related industries. At the same time the overheated and overpriced economy of southern England will push developments northward searching for lower-cost, less congested locations that offer better quality of life in attractive surroundings. From this there could well be economic benefits for parts of the county from footloose and high-technology industrial and commercial projects. How to use this growth potential to help the inner city and the former mining areas will be a major challenge. The decision of the Toyota Motor Corporation to establish a vehicle assembly plant at Burnaston near Derby, to serve the European market, will dramatically boost the economic prospects of the county, both directly through 3,000 new jobs at the plant, and indirectly through related spin-off development.

The geology of Derbyshire has provided both attractive landscape and mineral wealth. The problems associated with protecting the former and exploiting the latter will increase. Visitor pressure on fine countryside will intensify as personal mobility extends, and leisure and tourist activities boom. Demands for more access to the countryside will require careful and sensitive management of resources to avoid the despoliation of that which people seek to enjoy. New and innovative leisure complexes will relieve some of the pressure and provide new employment, but public concern over environmental pollution will continue to increase...

Councillor Martin Doughty, Chair of Planning and Countryside Committee

greenfield location
Sites outside existing urban areas which are not already cluttered by commercial developments. Given good communications, many firms look for such locations to build headquarters, research buildings, computer centres, etc. These then enjoy an attractive 'campus' or college-style environment.

LEICESTERSHIRE COUNTY COUNCIL

The face of Leicestershire in the 1990s is likely to be shaped by a range of new developments. If *economic growth* continues at the pace experienced in recent years, there will be more pressure to release land. This will be for development at highly accessible and **greenfield locations** to meet the needs of high-tech industry and offices requiring 'campus style' facilities with adequate parking.

In terms of *transportation* there are likely to be more vehicles in the next decade, causing further congestion problems. Important road programmes for the '90s include the A1–M1 link, the M42/A42 from the West Midlands to the M1, and the A564 Stoke–Derby link. Public transport thinking includes new rail services which may attract some car users from busy roads.

Most importantly, in relation to the *countryside* in the next decade, the County Council has prepared the plan 'Countryside 2000'. This recognises the many demands which are placed on the countryside and the sometimes conflicting expectations about its use. The demand for countryside leisure is growing and some Leicestershire attractions are already suffering from congestion. The plan tries to meet these needs while considering those of people living and working there.

T. W. Thompson, Director of Planning and Transportation

Lincolnshire County Council

Director of Highways and Planning
J Emmerson BSc MSc PhD CEng MICE

The principal challenge facing Lincolnshire in the 1990s is the challenge of change. Traditionally regarded as a rural backwater dominated by agriculture, the County has recently been 'discovered' and is now experiencing rapid population growth. Farming, of course, remains of vital importance with over $1\frac{1}{2}$ million acres of prime agricultural land. However, even here, changes can be expected as national policies begin to play down the traditional supremacy of agricultural needs.

Rapid increases in net in-migration suggest Lincolnshire's population could reach 673,000 by the year 2001—15 per cent greater than in 1988. Over 50,000 new homes will be needed for this and their sensitive location is one of the key issues to be faced. House prices in Lincolnshire have risen very sharply. There is now the emerging problem of local people, particularly the young, being unable to afford housing in their home area.

It is important that communications with the rest of the country are improved. In the longer term there is support for a possible M11 extension through the County from the South East to the Humber Bridge and the North. Better communications are a key factor in the attraction of new industry which is needed to replace jobs lost in the traditional occupations of agriculture and heavy engineering.

Finally and unusually, Lincolnshire faces both the problems and the opportunities provided by mineral extraction. The County is now the second largest producer of onshore oil nationally and there are immense coal reserves (about 180 million tonnes) awaiting exploitation in the Witham Prospect between Lincoln and Newark.

Lincolnshire is rightly famous for the openness of its skies and countryside. Perhaps the greatest challenge of all is to ensure that as the County enters an era of new and varied development, this unique environment is not seriously damaged.

J. Emmerson, Director of Highways and Planning

de-industrialisation
Decline in the importance of manufacturing industry within a country's economy. Usually measured in terms of reduced employment in manufacturing and lower relative value of output.

commuter
A person who lives at some distance from his or her workplace and therefore travels regularly between the two locations.

Northamptonshire

It can be argued that Northamptonshire forms part of the East Midlands more for administrative convenience than because of any common geographical feature. Thus, while planners throughout the region face issues like environmental pollution, increasing travel, agricultural productivity, **de-industrialisation**, leisure growth and demographic structure, in Northamptonshire we now have to reconsider the planning implications of our geographical position. Northamptonshire is often regarded as being at the crossroads of England... and it is now within easy reach of all parts of the country. Significantly, much of the County is within an hour's drive or an hour's train journey of London (which is much less than for most of the rest of the East Midlands). Pressure for homes for **commuters** and for industrial and commercial development is thus closely related to a perception of Northamptonshire's shrinking 'distance' from the capital.

The recently approved County Structure Plan recognises some of the implications of this changing role. It endeavours to allow for new opportunities to be seized whilst protecting the attractive environment which has in itself contributed to the development pressures. During the 1990s many of these pressures will change. By then, Northamptonshire may well be seen (by those with whom it has significant economic links) as forming part of London's hinterland rather than as part of the 'industrial Midlands'. Our future choices may therefore be limited in new and unexpected ways.

Michael J. Kendrick, Director of Planning and Transportation

A major issue facing Nottinghamshire in the 1990s will be the prospects for the economy, including the future of the coal industry and mining employment. (The industry had 18,500 workers in 1989, having lost 22,500 jobs in the previous nine years.) The proportion of jobs in services is likely to increase further, including tourism where growth may have a significant impact on the landscape.

The privatisation of the electricity supply could have some notable local effects, including the building of 'mini' power stations rather than the major structures now found along the River Trent. Pressures for 'dispersal' could bring more retail, leisure and business park development away from town and city centres. Less concentration of population could also result from more working and shopping from home and growing perception of the attractions of life in small towns like Newark and East Retford. However, policies to protect the green belt and open country are likely to remain strong.

Last but not least is the issue of transport strategy in face of growing traffic congestion, limited resources and the needs of those without private transport. We might expect, for example, pressures both for more by-passes and a resurgence of public transport based on new technologies.

Vivian Payne, Director of Planning and Transportation

1 Make a list under county headings of the changes that the planners predict.
2 Identify those changes that you think will involve people disagreeing over the way in which land should be used in the East Midlands.
3 Produce your own list of changes and land use issues that you think will be important in your area in the 1990s.

Summary

- The region's planners suggest that various trends and issues will influence life and landscape in the East Midlands by the end of this century. They point to changes in population structure, employment and leisure patterns, transport, the use of agricultural land, demands on open space, the high cost of land and housing. They stress the difficulty of balancing further economic development with the urgent need to conserve the environment. In this book we have used the geographer's viewpoint to try to make better sense of living space and lifestyles in the East Midlands. We hope it will help you in your future of choices wherever you live.

Index

Page numbers in italics refer to tables or illustrations.

agriculture, *see* farming
air services, 51–3
Alfreton, *13*, 19
Angles and Saxons, 14–16
Anglian Water, 23, 30–1
Areas of outstanding natural beauty (AONB), 83
Arkwright, Richard, 61–2
Asfordby, 41
Ashby, *4*, *40*, *49*, 86

Band Aid, 57
baseflow, 32–3
Blyth, 47
Bolsover, *6*, *7*, 25, *37*
Boston, *4*, *6*, *7*, *13*, *20*, 45–6, *49*, 54, *66*, 69
British Coal Corporation, 40–3
British Midland Airways (BMA), 51–3
British Rail (BR), 48–50
British Telecom, 5, 6, 78
Buxton, *4*, *13*, *49*, 54, 69, *85*

canals, 35, 46–7, 83
Carboniferous rocks, 31, 32, *37*
cartography, 10
Castle Donington, *40*, 51
Center Parcs, 88–9
Central Business District (CBD), 71–5
Central Place Theory, 70–2
Central Statistical Office (CSO), 5
Chapel St Leonards, 27
Charnwood Forest, 23, *24*, 83
Chesterfield, *4*, *6*, *7*, *13*, 26, 35, *37*, *40*, *49*, *50*, *66*, 85
climate/weather, 14, 28–33
coaching, 47
coal industry, 37–43, 92
Coal Measures, *9*, 23, 37–43, 92
Coalville, *13*, 43, 69
Common Agricultural Policy (CAP), 55–60
Common Market, 55–60, 91
commuters, 93
concealed coalfield, *37*, *38*
conservation/conservationists, 59, 87, 91–3
conurbation, 19
Corby, *4*, *6*, *7*, *13*, *49*, 62–3, 65, *66*
core and frame, 73–4
core-periphery model, 19–21
correlation, 67
corridor of growth, 19

cottage industry, 61
County Structure Plans, 90–3
Country Parks, *83*, 86
Cranwell, 10–11, 23–7
Cresswell Crags, 13–14
Cromford, 61–2
cultural landscape, 13
cumulative causation, 19

Danes and Norsemen, 14–16
Dark Peak, *24*, *28*, 86
data interpretation, 5–8
Daventry, *4*, *6*, *7*, *49*, *66*, 70
decision-making, 68, 91
de-industrialisation, 64–8, 93
demography, 21
Derby, *4*, *6*, *7*, 10, 11, *13*, 17, *33*, *38*, *40*, *48*, *49*, *50*, *51*, *52*, 64–7, 73, *85*, 91
Derbyshire, *4*, 5–7, 21, 35–7, 55, 57, 81–3, 86, 91
Derbyshire Wildlife Trust, 87
derelict land, 42–3
Derwent, River, *4*, 23, *24*, *33*, 73, 83
Derwent Reservoirs, 23, 26, *33*
Dove, River 23
Dronfield, *13*

earnings, 18, *20*, 82
East Lindsey, *6*, *7*, *66*, 84
East Midlands International Airport (EMIA), 10, 51–3
East Midlands Tourist Board (EMTB), 5, 86
East Retford, *13*, 27, *38*, *40*, *50*, 70, 93
Eastwood, 9
ecology/ecosystem, *28*, 88
electoral register, 6
employment, *20*, 38–9, 47, 53, 54, *57*, 61–7, 70, 88, 91–3
energy, 38–44, 61–2, 92–3
entrepreneur, 35
environment, 13–15, *28*, 35–6, 41–4, 55–9, 61–7, 83–7, 91–3
 changes in, 13–15, 35–6, 55–9, 61–7, 91–3
 protection of, *28*, 41–4, 59, 83–7, 91–3
 recreational, *28*, 83–7, 91–3
Erewash River/Valley, *9*, *24*
ethnic minorities, 16–18, 65–6, 76
European Community (EC), 55–60
exposed Coal Measures, 35, *37*

factory system, 61–2
farming, 54–60, 91–3
 areas of, *54*
 changes in, 55–7, 91–3
 political factors in, 55–60
 systems of, 55–6
Fens, 5, 23, *24*, 27
food mountain, 57
formal regions, 5
Fossdyke, 46, *47*, 83
Fosse Way, 11
free market, 55
functional regions, 5

Gainsborough, *7*, *13*, *47*, 70
General Election 1987, 6, *7*
geographical distribution, 12
geological time-scale, *31*
Glossop, *4*, *13*, 70
goods/services, 70–2
 classification of, 71
 clustering of, 71–2
government policies, 29, 40, 53, 59–60, 63, 68
Grantham, *4*, *7*, *13*, 42, *47*, *49*, 70
Great North Road, *47*
greenfield location, 92
groundwater, 32–3

Hinckley, *4*, *6*, *13*, *49*, *66*, 70
hinterland, 46
Hope Valley, *26*, *85*
Horncastle, *7*, 27
house prices, 80–1, 92
'hub and spoke' centres, 52
hydrology, 23, 29–33

Ice Age, 13
Ilkeston, 35
images of place, 8–9
immigration, 14–18
impermeable marl, 32
industrial revolution, 35, 61–2
industry, 35–44, 61–8
 changes in, 35–44, 64–8, 91–3
 classification of, 64, 91–3
 location of, 35–41, 62–8, 91–3
 inner city, 65–7, 75–6
iron and steel, 35–7, 62–3
Ironville, 37

jobs / job losses, 41, 42, 47, 53, 61–8, 83, 88, 91–3

95

Kegworth, 48
Kettering, *4, 6, 7,* 11, *13, 49, 50,* 65, 66, *70*
Kinder Scout, 26

land use, 54–5, 71–4, 91–4
landscape/landforms, 9, 13–15, 23–8, 83–7
Lawrence, D. H., 9
Leicester, *4, 6, 7,* 10, *11,* 13, *17, 33, 38,* 45, *48, 49, 50, 51, 52,* 66, 71–2, *76, 77, 78*
Leicestershire, *4,* 5–7, *21,* 36, *55, 57,* 81–3, *86,* 92
leisure/tourism, 80–9, 91–3
Lincoln, *4, 6, 7,* 10, *11,* 13, 15, 27, *48, 49, 50, 51, 52,* 66, 92
Lincoln Edge, *4,* 23, 24, 69
Lincolnshire, *4,* 5–7, 10–11, *17, 21,* 36, *55, 57, 77, 78,* 81–3, *86,* 92
Lincolnshire Wolds, *4,* 14, *24,* 83
Lindon/Lindum Colonia, 15
liner services, 46
local authority areas, 6–7
location, 45–6, 50, 69, 72, 88, 91–3
  least-cost/optimal, 62–3
  principles of industrial, 62
Long Eaton, 33, 70, 86
Loughborough, *4, 7,* 13, *49, 70*
Louth, *4,* 13, *49, 70*

Mablethorpe, *4, 84*
Manpower Services Commission (MSC), 68
Mansfield, *4, 6, 7,* 9, *13,* 38, *49,* 85
manufacturing, 61–3, 91–3
Market Harborough, *4, 49, 70*
Matlock, *4,* 9, *13, 49, 50,* 69, *70,* 85
Matlock Bath, 35, 87
Melton Mowbray, *4,* 13, 42, 66, *70*
mineral resources, 36–7
mining, 24–5, 35–43, 91–3
motorways, 25, 48, 49, 92

National Coal Board (NCB), 40
National Nature Reserves (NNRs), 86
National Union of Mineworkers (NUM), 40
nationalisation, 38
natural change, 21
Nature Conservancy Council (NCC), 86
Nene, River, *4,* 14, 23, 24, 31, *83*
networks/nodes, 46–52
Newark, *4, 6, 7,* 11, *13,* 38, *40, 49,* 50, 69
Normans, 14–16
Northampton, *4, 6, 7,* 11, *13,* 38, *48, 49, 50, 52,* 63, *66,* 72
Northamptonshire, *4,* 5–7, *17, 21,* 36, *55, 57,* 65, *67, 79,* 81–3, *86,* 93

Northamptonshire Uplands, *24*
Nottingham, *4, 6, 7,* 10, *11,* 13, *17,* 18, *20, 33, 40,* 45, *47,* 48, *49, 50, 51, 52,* 66, 73–5, *85*
Nottinghamshire, *4,* 5–7, *17, 21, 33,* 36, *55, 57,* 81–3, *86,* 91

Oakham, 69
occupations, 7, 64–7, 70, 91–3
oil production, 92
Ollerton, 25, 37, *40*
opencast mining, 43
Oundle, *70*

parliamentary constituencies, 6, 7
Peak District, 5, 28, *83,* 85–6
Peak National Park, 28, 85–7
pedestrian flows, 72
Pennine Way, 83
perception, 8–9, 14–15, 18, 93
place-names, 15
planning, 42–3, 85, 91–3
political parties, 6–7, 29, 40–1, 53, 55–60, 63
population, 7, 13, 19, 21, 79
  changes/trends in, 21, 79
population gradient, 19
ports, 45–6
poverty, 66–7
power stations, 38–41
prairie farming, 59
primary industry, 64, 91
privatisation, 29, 40–1, 53
productivity, 56
public enquiries, 42
public sector, 29
push-pull model, 16–18

railways, 47–50, 84
  contraction of, 48
  cross-country services, *51,* 84
  passenger flows, *49*
  journey times, *50*
rainfall, 30, 31–3
random distribution, 12
regime, 32
regional trends, 6–8
remote sensing, 10
retailing, 72–3
roads, 45–9, 91–3
rock types, 23, 31–2, 36–7
Rockingham Forest, 24
Rolls Royce, 64
Romans, 14–15, 35, 45, 46, 47
rural problems, 77–8
Rutland Water, 23, *83*

Scunthorpe, 61
sea defences, 30
seaside resorts, 84
secondary industry, 64

Sence, River, *32*
services, 64, 69–78
settlements, 13–15, 69–70, 91–3
  hierarchy of, 70
  patterns of, 13–14
  types of, 69
Severn-Trent Water, 23, 31–3
Sherwood Forest, 9, *24,* 25, *83*
Sherwood Forest Holiday Village, 88–9
Sites of Special Scientific Interest (SSSIs), 86
Skegness, 10, *13, 49,* 69, *84*
skill training, 67–8
Sleaford, *13,* 86
Snake Pass, 26
Snibston, *40,* 43
Soar, River, *4, 24,* 33, *47*
Southwell, *70*
Spalding, *4,* 10, *13, 49, 70*
sphere of influence, 69
Stamford, *4,* 13, *47, 49*
Standard Regions, 5
superstores, 72
surface runoff, 32
Sutton in Ashfield, *70*
Swadlincote, *13, 70*

tertiary sector, 64, 69–74
textiles, 61–2, 64–5
tourism/leisure, 80–9
Towcester, 69
Toyota Motor Corporation, 64, 91
transport, 45–53, 85, 93
Trent Navigation, 46–7, 83
Trent, River, *4,* 23, *24,* 26, *46, 47, 83,* 93
turnpikes, 47

unemployment, 65–8, *76,* 91, 93
Union of Democratic Mineworkers (UDM), 40
urban deprivation, 66–7
urban field, 69
urban functions, 69–70
urban renewal, 73–5
urban structure, 73–5

Vale of Belvoir, 41–2

Wash, The, 10, *11, 24, 31*
water services, 29–33
Welland, River, *4,* 14, 23, *24,* 83
Wellingborough, *6, 7,* 13, *49,* 66, *70*
Whistlestop Countryside Centre, 87
White Peak, *24,* 28
Witham, River, *4,* 23, *24,* 27, *33,* 83
Witham Gap, 27
Witham Prospect, 92
Woodhall Spa, 27
Wreake, River, *83*
Worksop, *4,* 13, 27, *49, 70*
Wye, River, *32*